THE COMPLETE HANDBOOK OF
OF
Dog Training

THE COMPLETE HANDBOOK
OF
Dog Training

Thomas A. Knott
with
Dolores Oden Cooper

HOWELL
BOOK HOUSE
New York

Macmillan General Reference
A Simon & Schuster Macmillan Company
1633 Broadway
New York, NY 10019-6785

Library of Congress Cataloging-in-Publication Data

Knott, Thomas A.
    The complete handbook of dog training / by Thomas A. Knott and
Dolores Oden Cooper.
        p. cm.
    ISBN 0-87605-555-2
    1. Dogs—Training. I. Cooper, Dolores Oden.   II. Title.
SF431.K57 1993   93-14573 CIP
636.7'0887—dc20

10 9 8 7 6 5

Printed in the United States of America

Dedicated to Mary Jean
and ''Gretchen''
Einsam Gretchen of Bourbon, UD,
who trained us both

T.A.K.

I dedicate this book to my husband Larry,
with love and appreciation for his many
contributions and unfailing support.

D.O.C.

About the Author

Tom Knott has been involved in the sport of dog training since childhood when he helped his grandfather, a professional bird dog trainer. He has actively worked in water training, training scent hounds and bird dogs for the field, Obedience and Tracking. He has been a member of the Obedience Advisory Council for the American Kennel Club and is an AKC Conformation, Obedience, Tracking and Advanced Tracking judge. He is a former president of the Association of Obedience Clubs and Judges of America, Inc., and the training director of the Dog Owner's Training Club of Maryland, Inc. (a position he has held for over thirty years). He is also the club's delegate to AKC. Tom and his wife, Mary Jean, have bred Weimaraners and German Shepherd Dogs. They have personally shown a total of seventeen Weimaraners to AKC championships. Moreover, Tom has trained numerous handlers to train dogs to their Utility and CDX titles.

Tom was the Training Director of the Baltimore City Police Department's K-9 Corps for over fifteen years. He is considered to be one of the country's outstanding authorities on the training of K-9 dogs for police work, narcotics and bomb detection. He has lectured widely on the use of dogs in law enforcement, and provided specialized training to K-9 units of the U.S. Navy, Coast Guard and hostage retrieval teams of the FBI and the White House, to name a few. He is currently an expert witness on dogs in police work and tracking. He is qualified to testify in federal and state courts.

Tom has worked on olfaction and scent discrimination studies using canines with the Sloan Kettering Cancer Institute and the Johns Hopkins Applied Physics Laboratory. He has written the foreword to The American Rescue Dog Association's prestigious new book *Search and Rescue Dogs—Training Methods* (Howell, 1991).

Dolores Oden Cooper attended Seton Hall University in New Jersey. She was director of continuity at WAAT-WATV in Newark, and an advertising copywriter in New York. In addition, for a number of years, she did publicity and public relations for art organizations. She is herself an artist, and contributed the diagrams for the exercises throughout the book. At present she is working as a free-lance writer and illustrator.

Contents

UTILITY TRAINING

Acknowledgments

Our sincere thanks go out to the many people who contributed in so many generous ways to this book.

A special thank you goes to the members of Dog Owners Training Club of Maryland, Inc., for their help and assistance whenever it was needed.

To Jim Dearinger, vice-president of Obedience and Tracking for the AKC, a very special thank you for his many kindnesses.

We are especially indebted to Dr. Larry Cooper for his belief in the concept of this book and his enthusiastic and tireless contribution to its preparation.

We would like to thank H. Melvin Volkert, Jr., for his wonderful photographs. He is an instructor at DOTC and a friend of many years. He is the official photographer for the Baltimore Colt Band and worked as an industrial photographer for Westinghouse.

Many thanks as well to Dorothy L. W. Redding, the very talented artist responsible for the beautiful line drawings. She depicts wildlife for the National Wildlife Federation, the Audubon Society and the Alaskan Malamute Annual. One of her dog paintings hangs in the Dog

Museum of America in St. Louis. She has had exhibits at the Museum of Art in Baltimore and galleries in the area.

We are grateful to the talented and very computer-literate Thad Cooper, for all his computer support work during the preparation of our manuscript.

We wish to thank the AKC for permission to reproduce sections taken from the Obedience Regulations book.

To Dr. Gail Smith, veterinary surgeon and researcher on hip dysplasia at the University of Pennsylvania, thank you for providing current information on hip dysplasia research.

And, finally, we would like to express our sincere appreciation to Marcy Zingler, our senior editor at Howell, for her kindness and expertise.

Foreword

TOM KNOTT and I first met at the Bryn Mawr Kennel Club show in June 1973. While we were talking, I was approached by a serious-minded Tracking enthusiast who wanted the answer to a difficult question on Tracking procedures. Frankly, I had no ready answer.

I knew instantly that Tom was aware of my predicament. Without hesitation, he answered the question as though it were addressed to him. Then he turned to me and said, without batting an eye, "Oh, sorry, Jim. I should have let you answer that." From that moment on we became friends, and we continue to be friends to this day. Over the years, I came to know Tom's love of dogs and his great knowledge and talent as a trainer. He is, indeed, a remarkable man and a credit to the world of dogs.

As I look at this book, I am reminded of John Brownell, assistant to the chief executive officer of the AKC from 1955 until he retired as vice president in 1972. John was known for his logic, his clear writing and expert editing of the AKC's rules, regulations and policies. Obedience was his primary interest. In the early years of AKC and Obedience, he wrote that training is *progressive*. Tom Knott, in this book, speaks of the "building blocks" to training.

Whatever the reference, no matter what it is called, the desired goals are the same. Tom, in this book, demonstrates an organized, progressive overview, coupled with great sensitivity in his training methods and techniques, and has successfully, I feel, conveyed this message to all who are interested in the training of the dog. He contends that by using caring and sensible methods of training, we not only make our dogs good citizens, but also strengthen the bond between man and dog. Those of us who have trained a dog know that good training results in a well-behaved companion, one who bothers neither the neighbors nor their dogs. The well-behaved dog does not balk at grooming procedures or a veterinarian's examination.

Training stimulates intelligence, and lends stability and meaning to the dog's life. This dog knows what is expected and works for your approval. Tom has captured the spirit of training and the fact that praise will mean so much to the dog, that pleasing you will encourage your dog to work from the heart and will bring out the best in your best friend.

For the first-time dog owner, this book is a must. However, it should be required reading not only for beginners, but for the advanced trainer as well.

James E. Dearinger
Vice-President, American Kennel Club
New York, New York

Preface

TRAINING THE BUILDING BLOCKS

It has been my experience that people, by and large, have a tendency to want to move their dogs along too quickly in training. They don't want to follow a structured training program consistently, because they feel their dog is especially quick to learn and therefore doesn't need the amount of time or reinforcement suggested. This is a mistake that can make problems for both the handler and the dog.

You will do better if you have a long-range view of dog training. There are "building blocks" that the dog learns in the most basic training that are used throughout Novice, Open and Utility. Think of them as the foundation of a successful training program. As you can imagine, it is crucial to this success that you take the time to teach them thoroughly and reinforce them sufficiently.

These include the Sit, Down and Stand. The Come command must be included here as well. The dog should learn to Take and Give toys and dumbbells early in training, and, of course, Heeling is fundamental. All these elements, combined in different ways, make up the more advanced exercises. How well your dog is able to perform them *with consistency* will affect the quality of your training not only in Novice, but in Open and Utility as well. Therefore, *be thorough in teaching and reinforcing them so that your "building blocks" don't turn into "stumbling blocks."*

You will also come across the term "unintentional training." It is a concept that is relatively simple, but until you become aware of what it is and how it can interfere with what you teach your dog, it can cause you problems that you believe are the dog's fault. In reality, *unintentional training* is the culprit.

The very term "unintentional training" should help you realize that, while it is happening, the handler is unaware of the problem that he or she is creating.

This book will make you more aware of what you are doing as you progress through KPT, Novice, Open and Utility training. It is a practical book, based on more than thirty years of dog training experience. I know that as you train and as you draw on this experience, you will come to recognize unintentional training and better understand how to prevent it from creeping into your training routine.

Introduction

THE MATERIAL contained in this book is largely a distillation of all my training methods that gradually developed during more than thirty years of dog training experiences, in Obedience classes, in clinics and in judging assignments, as well as during my work on the AKC advisory council on Obedience and Tracking. Whether totally spontaneous ideas or methods that have taken years to perfect, all of them reflect the philosophy that dog Obedience training should be a most enjoyable experience.

Enjoy dog training! Your dog is your best friend and should be treated *like a friend*. When your dog offers you complete trust and willingness to learn, respond in kind. It's your responsibility, and your joy, I hope, to learn how to teach your dog and to teach your dog how to learn.

To quote from the first page of the Regulations for The American Kennel Club Licensed Obedience Trials:

> *The performance of the dog handler in the ring must be accurate and correct and must conform to the requirements of these regulations. However, it is also essential that the dog demonstrate a willingness and enjoyment of its work, and smoothness and naturalness on the part of the handler are to be preferred to a performance based on military precision and peremptory commands.*

It has been my goal in this book to present training methods that not only meet the letter of the law as set down by the AKC, but also embrace the spirit of it as well. It is my contention that by using caring and sensible methods of training, we not only make our dogs good citizens, but also strengthen the bond of affection between ourselves and our dogs. Through the application of this philosophy, dog Obedience training can realize its full potential and enjoy the deep respect and admiration so earned.

Kindergarten Puppy Training (KPT)

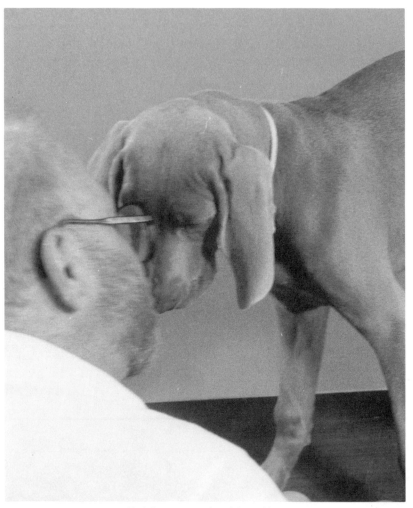
Training a puppy is a labor of love.

1

Introduction to KPT

$\mathbf{B}$EFORE YOU BEGIN training your dog, I encourage
you to read the entire book rather than a particular section that might
be of special interest at the moment. By reading the entire book, you
will begin to understand that you are working with an overall plan
consisting of a number of "building blocks." These are techniques
and instructions that may be developed at the KPT or Novice level,
but that will work for you at the Open or Utility level as well. You
will come to see that by looking at the larger picture, you can avoid
many problems of unintentional training that require retraining at a
later date.

KINDERGARTEN PUPPY TRAINING

Kindergarten Puppy Training, for the three-to-six-month-old
puppy, is the foundation of Obedience training. It is here that the basic
building blocks are put in place. By keeping the overall training picture
in mind, you will realize why working with such a young puppy is so
worthwhile.

However, to train a puppy this young, it takes understanding and
patience, patience, patience! Learning time should be a happy time for

the puppy, but it should also be presented a little differently from the free and easy fun-and-games time enjoyed with the family.

The challenge to you is to teach the fundamentals in a way that the puppy can understand. Your instructions must be clear. The whole experience should be a positive one filled with plenty of praise and encouragement. Avoid criticism and negative corrections. You don't want to create stubbornness, mental blocks or any of the other handling errors that fall under the heading of unintentional training, the chronic headache of the handler. It is our job to show our puppies that it's fun to learn.

TEACHING YOUR DOG HOW TO LEARN

Training a puppy is a labor of love that requires patience, discipline and dedication on the part of the handler. It takes energy and an upbeat attitude. Don't work with your puppy if you've had a bad day that has left you tired, irritable and stressed. Wait until you can approach training in a calm, cheerful, controlled manner. Should you become stressed *while* training, stop and play with the puppy for a few minutes. Never intimidate or frighten your puppy with an angry sounding voice or abrupt, impatient handling. Have a few minutes of fun and relax. Then begin again.

Remember, you're tugging and pushing and repeating words that are meaningless to the puppy. Without a doubt, your pup has other thoughts about fun things to do during the first few training sessions. If you are able to keep that point of view in mind, it will really help you to be patient and remain calm. Your dog will get the idea and cooperate—eventually!

When you start with a very young puppy, be satisfied if the dog can get the exercise right even once or twice. When that happens give lots of praise and then stop for a short while before going on. Also, it's important to end training sessions on a high note that makes the puppy feel good. The pup will get the idea that training is fun and you'll be able to use that natural enthusiasm to hold interest and build confidence.

As you move along into more difficult exercises, always finish with something the dog already does well, then give plenty of praise. Your dog works for you to earn your smiles and approval. So don't be stingy with your praise for a good job. Let your dog hear all those wonderful, rewarding words.

4

THE LEARNING CURVE

You will find, as you train, that learning is not a matter of constant, steady improvement. The dog experiences a series of peaks and valleys as you both move along. This is simply the way the learning process works. Realize that, and you will be able to enjoy your training without feeling, from time to time, that you have the most backward dog in the universe!

Be prepared to be patient, gentle in the way you physically handle the puppy, and be soft spoken. Listen to yourself. This is important now and throughout *all of your training*. Whenever you are teaching a new exercise, NEVER raise your voice or give a "tough" correction. You are not being fair to the dog. This is fundamental to my method of training.

You cannot allow yourself to lose your temper. Loud, angry or demanding tones will frighten the puppy and seriously inhibit any ability to learn. If you have problems with your training and you think it might be the way you give commands, use a tape recorder and listen to yourself as you train. You can learn a lot that way.

Work at the puppy's level. Don't tower over the dog, issue sharp commands and expect immediate results. This is interpreted by the dog as intimidation. This destroys any sense of confidence and ability to focus and learn.

Your goal is to help the puppy *build confidence* and to find the training session a special time to be together and learn. This should be a time you both look forward to and that you both enjoy.

MOTIVATING YOUR DOG

I want to go on record as saying I am not a "food" trainer. I don't believe in it. Food reinforcement may seem like an attractive shortcut to get the dog to work, but in the long run, it isn't the most reliable or effective method. Think of training as a team effort. Develop a good relationship with your dog—a loving relationship. That should be the reason why your dog will work for you and try very hard to never let you down.

I've been training dogs for over fifty years. It has been my experience that the dog who is motivated by strong bonds of affection is the dog who gives you the best he or she has from within. Give *your* best to your dog and you can expect an equal effort in return. You don't

Attending class socializes the puppy while the handler benefits from experienced instruction.

need to bribe a dog with food to work. This is my belief, although I know there are people in dog training who disagree with this philosophy.

DOG SCHOOL VS. HOME SCHOOLING

Some people prefer to train their dogs at home. If this is your preference, try to work your dog occasionally where there are other dogs present. See if neighbors or friends might be willing to bring their dogs to your training sessions. If that doesn't work, seriously consider going to at least one course of training at the Novice level, where dogs have the opportunity to socialize and work in groups.

That way, the dog learns not to be intimidated by strangers, other dogs, unfamiliar noises or unexpected happenings. Another advantage of training in a class is that instructors spot handler error in posture, voice and method. These errors are an endless source of unintentional training.

However, if you decide to take the dog to school, attend a class before you sign up. Be sure the method of instruction offered is based on a caring philosophy, using praise as reinforcement and only as much correction as is necessary to get the job done. In my long experience, prong or spike collars, heavy-handed corrections or food reinforcement are not the way you want to go with your dog.

I should mention, however, that there are some dogs I would call "sharp dogs"—willful dogs who express themselves aggressively from puppyhood on. Here, I recommend a firm hand right from early puppyhood in order to get your point across. That doesn't mean heavy equipment or a heavy hand, however. It just means consistent, firm, *fair discipline*.

Always remember that these dogs need praise when they begin to respond. This is an important moment for these dogs. At the appropriate times, when they do well, you may find they need even more praise than the gentler dog. This will help to keep them properly motivated. However, this does not mean inappropriate gushing compliments that even *they* know is a con job.

IS IT EVER TOO LATE TO BEGIN?

KPT usually begins when the puppy is between three and six months of age. However, don't let the title of these exercises fool you. KPT is for *beginners* and *not* designed *exclusively* for the training of very young puppies. *Use the KPT exercises for dogs of any age if you are just starting their training.*

COLLARS AND LEADS—UNDER FOUR MONTHS OF AGE

For a puppy under four months of age, use a thin, inexpensive buckle collar made of three-eighths-inch soft, flat-braid nylon. The lighter, the better. Let the puppy wear it around the house to get used to it. Now, don't think that because the collar will last for such a short period of time it's a waste of money. The puppy will outgrow this collar, true, but this gentle introduction will accustom the puppy to the feel of it and will pay off in the long run.

It's not all that unusual for people to buy heavy, bulky leather collars and leads that all but outweigh the puppy, because they believe the dog will grow into them. That's like buying shoes for a six-month-old baby that will fit when the child is two years old.

Even if your puppy is large, lively or aggressive at this age only a lightweight type of collar is needed. A puppy should not have to drag around a heavy collar and lead so overpowering that your dog will start fighting it, which will create an unnecessary problem even before you start. In addition to the lightweight buckle collar, use a six-foot cotton web lead, no wider than one-half inch, when you begin walking your puppy. Be sure the snap swivel on the lead is lightweight as well.

2

The Young Puppy: Simple Exercises and Training Play

WHEN YOU BEGIN KPT training, find a place to work that is comfortable for you. If you have a small puppy, use a grooming table or a bench. Just make sure to put a piece of rug or mat on the surface so it isn't slippery.

For the large puppy, work on the floor, also on a nonskid surface. Kneel on the floor on your right knee and keep the left knee up. Kneeling this way creates an L-shaped area in front of you that helps keep the puppy positioned. Your dog fits in there next to your body, tail toward your left leg. The puppy's head is toward your right elbow. In this way, you can control even a lively puppy's movements.

When teaching the Stand, create a lower silhouette by sitting back on your foot. That way you don't tower over the puppy. Most puppies are intimidated by handlers hanging over them.

When you begin training, the Stand is an easy first exercise. You will then progress to the Sit and the Down exercises. The Stay command will be introduced as well.

The puppy initially is *assisted into position* and introduced to the appropriate word in a long, drawn-out manner—S-T-A-N-D, S-I-T and D-O-W-N. The puppy learns to associate the word with the action.

As you move the puppy through the exercises, give praise even though you are the one who moved the dog into position. This is important. It builds confidence as your puppy learns.

RELEASE WORD

It is also important, from the start, to have a release word or phrase that you use when you are done with the lesson. When finished, remove the lead first, and then after a second or two give the release word. One phrase that is commonly used is "All done." Once you give the release word, spend a few minutes playing with your dog.

THE THREE-IN-ONE

Although you will be teaching your puppy the Stand, Sit and Down as *separate* exercises when you first start training, you will find that they easily combine into a three-in-one routine as the puppy gets the hang of things. Therefore, although each exercise will be described in detail separately, once learned you can vary them in any combination. Variety prevents boredom and keeps the puppy's attention. Initially, if the puppy holds each position steadily for three to five seconds, you're doing well.

A suggested training schedule is five to ten minutes twice a day. Your goal at the end of KPT is, minimally, to have your puppy hold the three positions steadily for fifteen to thirty seconds. In addition your dog should be able to walk on-lead and do the KPT recall.

The KPT Stand

To begin teaching the Stand exercise, set the dog up in front of you, with the head toward your right elbow and the tail to your left. The first time you set the puppy up, expect to find yourself dealing with a bundle of playful energy. Work calmly to gain the pup's attention. Keep a happy expression on your face and your voice light. If you suddenly start glaring, growling, and pulling the puppy around, your dog will think he's done something wrong.

With your right hand, take hold of the back or side of the dog's

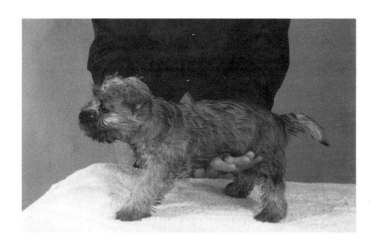

This 9 week old Cairn Terrier is being taught the KPT Stand, Sit and Stay. At this age and size, the puppy should be trained on a table covered with a non-skid surface. The handler must work slowly and gently.

11

collar. At the same time, place your left hand under the dog against the pup's back legs, palm facing downward. Say the dog's name and then give the Stand command. Stretch the word out like a rubber band. As you say "Stand," gently pull up and forward on the collar and *lightly* touch the dog's back leg. This moves the dog into the proper standing position. Don't hit against the leg, just use a light touch. Don't haul the dog up into a standing position either. As the puppy stands, keep your left hand in place against the rear leg. This helps to steady the puppy. Then tell the dog to Stay.

If you're training a larger breed, put a little more arm under your dog so you are touching both legs. That way, if the pup starts to move away, you can turn your hand up, palm facing outward on the far side to hold the dog in position. Reinforce the Stand command with one or more Stay commands for steadying.

When you give the Stay command, use your right hand. Keep the fingers of your right hand together, palm toward the dog's face, about four inches away. As you say "Stay," move your hand firmly an inch or two toward the face. Don't swing your hand as though you're going to hit the puppy's face. It's just a short, smooth movement with the flat of your hand that stops a few inches from the puppy's face.

As you give the verbal Stay command and hand signal, your left hand remains in place. Initially, try to hold the Stand position for at least several seconds. After you give the Stay command and your dog remains steady, be sure to praise. At this point you are ready to move into the Sit exercise.

The KPT Sit

You are beginning this exercise as the puppy stands with the head toward your right elbow. Hold the collar firmly with your right hand. Your left hand is still under the dog holding the dog in the Stand position. At this point, remove your left hand from under the puppy. Use the dog's name and give the Sit command. Draw out the command in a cheerful voice. With the edge of your left hand, push in at the back of the dog's knee on the hamstrings. The legs will fold into a sit. As you do this, use your right hand to pull the collar up and back slightly. Keep both movements *smooth and gentle*. Don't push the legs so that the dog crumbles—this is a puppy! As the dog sits, give the Stay command and hand signal. Then praise the puppy with enthusiasm.

Note that your left hand runs lightly down the puppy's back. The gentle stroking and praise is both reassuring and relaxing.

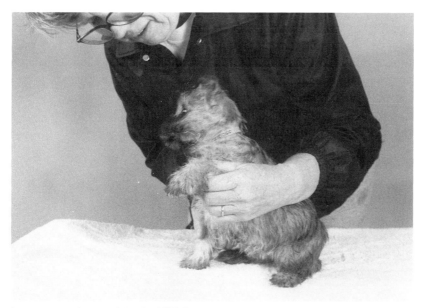

In step one, when teaching the KPT Down, it helps the puppy to relax if you raise and shake each leg.

The KPT Down

From the sitting position the Down command is introduced. Although dogs often lay around the house looking very content, most do not like being *forced* into this position. It is a problem to get the handler to really understand that dogs resist having their front legs pulled out from under them.

The exercise is easier to teach if you can help the dog to relax. When you work with the smaller dog on a table, reach around the pup's back with your left arm, lift one front leg up a few inches, shaking it gently up and down. Praise your dog for letting you raise the leg. Then gently place the leg down and lift the other leg with the right hand and shake it in the same way. Praise again in a quiet voice. This is your first step. It is simply a confidence builder for the dog that shows there is nothing to fear.

Step two will get both legs up together. Reach your left arm over the pup's back and take hold of the left leg; with your right hand take hold of the right leg. Gently raise both legs slightly off the table. Quietly say "What a good dog." If the puppy stiffens up, shake the held legs gently to loosen them up and relax them. When your dog relaxes, use praise again. Then, stretch those legs slightly forward and

13

In step two, get both legs up together, again shaking them gently if the puppy begins to stiffen up.

very gently place the dog down while using his name and giving the Down command.

If you're working on the floor, a large dog should be placed sitting in front of you, close to your body. Your dog's front end should be somewhat angled away from you to give you room to work. Brace your left foot firmly against the rump to keep everything in place while you put the dog into the Down position. If necessary, hold the collar with your right hand. With the left hand reach over the back and take hold of the dog's left front leg, lift it gently and shake it slowly up and down until the leg begins to relax. Keep moving the leg as you talk to the dog quietly. Next, let go of the collar and, with your right hand, take hold of the right leg. Hold it for a second or two before you lift it. That little moment of hesitation seems to keep the dog from being startled and stiffening up again.

Shake both legs up and down together slowly with a gentle rock-ing motion until you feel them relax. Then with your left arm around the dog, brace your elbow against the left hip and place your dog in the Down position. Don't stop rocking the front paws during the downward movement. While doing this use the dog's name and give

In step three, when relaxed the puppy's legs are stretched forward and very gently placed down.

the Down command very gently. Once the dog is down, run your left hand down his back. Give a Stay command and hand signal. Use a quiet voice so that the dog doesn't bob back up. Try to hold this position for three to five seconds to start. Your goal is to have the pup lay quietly, without the need for your hand on the dog's back. You can still steady with a Stay command and hand signal as necessary.

This method of teaching the dog to go down works very well. Don't try to get a puppy into the Down position by hovering and pushing down on the dog's head. The dog will resist, feeling resentful and helpless. The handler who tries to force a dog down creates unnecessary problems.

THREE-IN-ONE VARIATIONS

At this point, you are ready for the variations on the three-in-one concept. This is an important building block exercise. In addition to learning how to do the exercises well, because they are given in sequence, the puppy learns the rudiments of focus and attention.

Start by having the puppy Sit, Stand and Sit, in that order. Then try a Sit, Down and Sit, and next, a Sit, Down and Stand. You can use any variation, just don't keep repeating the exercises for too long a period of time. *The ability of a puppy to concentrate is limited*, just as is a child's.

If necessary, use plenty of Stay commands between the Sit, Stand or Down commands to help keep the puppy in position. Eliminate them when the puppy begins to perform reliably.

Work slowly. Be sure to pause between the commands. Don't run them together quickly. Draw out the command words slowly, and above all, move at a controlled, calm pace. Last but not least, never forget to sprinkle in a good helping of praise.

As the puppy begins to do well, *handlers tend to want to move along too quickly*. While it is true you want to minimize the cues, remember that it took the puppy time to learn from all these extra "helps." It is better to stop using them *gradually*. Taking these props out too soon will probably throw the dog into a state of confusion.

SAY HELLO TO THE LEAD

To introduce a puppy to the lead, use a short piece of cotton web lead with a lightweight snap swivel. I suggest the dog wear a quarter-inch collar made of soft, flat nylon. Fasten the lead to the collar.

Let the pup run about and get use to the feel of it for about twenty minutes at a time. Eventually your dog will forget about it and begin to scamper around in the usual playful way. Take the lead off when the "training session" is over. Never leave it on when the puppy is not supervised.

After a few days, the puppy should be used to the short lead. If not, don't hurry. Give as much time as needed for the pup to be comfortable with the feel of the lead before you begin working on a six-foot cotton web training lead.

Walking On-Lead

You will need a fair amount of space to begin to walk your dog on-lead, so I suggest you work outdoors. If this is not always possible, your basement or garage may provide a suitable alternative.

How you hold the lead will make a big difference in how well your dog will begin walking on-lead. The handler should have the lead under total control. If you're a beginning trainer, try practicing with someone holding on to the lead before your actually attach it to the puppy.

How to Hold the Lead Properly

Hang the loop of a six-foot lead on your right thumb and close your fingers around the loop. This gives you a firm grip on the lead. Holding the loop, raise your right hand about waist high. With your left hand, take hold of the lead below the right hand and slide it about one-third of the way down the lead. Then fold that one-third of the lead into loops slightly larger than the width of your palm and hold the folds in the right hand.

This enables you to take up some extra lead or let some out as necessary. Even if all the lead drops out of your hand, or the puppy pulls it out your hand, you've still got a hold on the loop. Your dog won't get away from you if you handle the lead this way. As you work, let enough lead hang down so that the snap swivel, attached to the collar, is hanging downward.

The left hand holds the lead at the side. Keep your left arm from the shoulder to the elbow close to your body. Keep your hand below the waist. Getting used to your hand down there ensures that the puppy won't become hand shy.

At this point, continue using a buckle collar. A young puppy under four months of age should not be on a slip collar. First of all, the neck is still tender, and the bones are soft. If you were to overreact and give a sharp correction, you could injure the puppy.

Talk in a gentle tone of voice as you attach the lead. Reassure your pup that it is *okay*. Once the lead is on, as the dog starts to move, you should move along also. Hold the lead loosely, without any tension on the collar. Accommodate yourself to the puppy at this point. Remember, this is just *walking on-lead*. You're not Heeling yet. You're getting the puppy used to the lead. Maneuver the dog to your left side. Watch your foot work. Don't flap your feet around. Keep them low to the ground and straight. You don't want to kick or hit the puppy with your feet because of sloppy footwork.

Talk in order to continually keep your dog moving with you. If he gets the lead tangled around your leg or around his legs, stop, kneel down and slowly untangle the lead. Call the dog's name, speak gently so as not to frighten your puppy. Once untangled, the puppy may be reluctant to continue walking. If this occurs, take a few steps away, and still holding the lead, call the dog's name, encouraging the pup to come. Give a gentle tug on the lead if necessary. When your dog responds and begins to follow you, praise as if this were something wonderful and continue talking as you move along. Keep the dog walking on your left side.

The pattern you follow is not too important, just try to change direction periodically. Turn to the left or right to keep the dog interested. Make curves rather than squared-off-turns. Make your steps small. As you turn, say the dog's name and "Heel." If the dog gets out of position as you walk along, try going in the opposite direction. Give gentle commands. Make your turns slowly. If your puppy doesn't understand when you say his name and give the Heel command, add a signal with your hand. You can pat your leg, for instance, or sweep your hand in the direction you want the puppy to follow. Corrections with the lead at this point are minimal.

After becoming used to the lead and staying at your side, have the puppy sit when you stop walking. Stop, then use the puppy's name and give the command Sit. If the dog doesn't sit, *don't* press on the back or rump to push the puppy down. Just tuck the rear under, the way you did when you taught the Sit exercise.

With practice, your dog will sit when you stop walking. These may not be perfect sits. Don't expect too much yet.

You have now reached a point at which your footwork becomes extremely important. You must *always step off on the left foot* after you give the Heel command. *This is the foot that guides your dog.* When your left foot moves, your puppy learns to move. *This is one of those building blocks*! Later on, when you move off on your right foot in the more advanced exercises, your dog knows to stay in place.

Left foot, the dog moves with you.
Right foot, the dog stays in place.

It is also a good idea to make that first step after the Heel command a *small step*, a half-step, so the puppy has time to get up and keep up with you.

Don't let the puppy mouth or chew at the lead while walking. Gently remove it, but don't pull it. This will turn into a tug-of-war game. Hold the lead up properly. If the lead is out of the way of the puppy's face, your dog will have a harder time getting hold of it.

KPT Corrections On-Lead

When the puppy understands walking on-lead and you begin to heel, you are ready to give *gentle corrections* when necessary. **Never give strong corrections to the dog when you are teaching a new exercise.** This is fundamental to my method of training. When learning an exercise, the dog does not yet know what you want. Therefore, he does not deserve strong corrections. On the other hand, don't give in to the dog who is being stubborn or sharp.

Correction at this time is simply to help keep the dog with you, to coordinate both your movements. For the very young dog, give *gentle* corrections. Keep your left elbow close to your side, holding the lead. Just turn the left wrist and lift the lead slightly with a little twisting motion. That is a sufficient correction at this time.

KPT SIT/STAY

After the puppy has learned the Sit, Stand and Down exercises and has been introduced to the lead, there is another exercise that we teach.

Put the puppy on-lead. Give the Sit and Stay command, and starting with your *right foot*, take a few steps and turn and face the puppy. Encourage the puppy to "S-t-a-a-y" in a cheerful voice. Include a Stay hand signal. Slowly increase the distance until you go to the end of the lead.

Go back to the puppy after a few seconds. Eventually work up to fifteen or even thirty seconds. When you return to the dog, walk around behind going to the Heel position so the dog is on your left side. Be careful how you handle the lead. The dog should not get hit in the face or feel the lead tighten or get tangled in it.

Praise enthusiastically if your dog does well. If puppy doesn't understand what you want or just wants to get over to you, gently put your dog back in place and again say "Stay." Make your voice light. Don't scold. Don't say no. *Only say what you want the pup to do— not what you don't want.* Talk as you work to hold attention, and your puppy will catch on quickly. As the dog gets it right, give plenty of praise. This is an important building block exercise that follows you through Novice, Open and Utility. Teach it well.

KPT RECALL

For this exercise, walk with the puppy on-lead. Then step back a few paces and gently pull the lead, pulling the puppy toward you. Say the puppy's name and give the Come command. You want to have the puppy sit in front of you.

Be sure your voice sounds inviting. If the pup is reluctant to move toward you, take a step or two backward and clap your hands. As your dog gets close to you, hold your hands out in front of you at ankle, calf or knee height depending upon the size of your puppy. Cup them as though you were holding a bubble. Again, depending on the size of the puppy, raise your "bubble" slowly up toward your waist. Raise it high enough so he looks up into your face. Move your hands slowly, as you want the dog's eyes to follow your hands. Usually, when eyes are looking that far upward, a dog's hindquarters will go down automatically into a sit. Praise enthusiastically.

If the dog looks up but doesn't sit, assist by tucking in the pup's rear as you draw back on the lead exactly as you did when teaching the Sit exercise.

Be sure that the puppy does *not* come when you say his *name*, but rather on the Come *command*. If the puppy comes to you without the command the first time, play a bit, then start again.

This is another of those building block exercises that will follow through Novice, Open and Utility. Take the time to teach it correctly.

KPT JUMPING

At this point, add a little jump exercise. This KPT jumping exercise is usually introduced at the beginning of the fourth week. Not only will this exercise break up any feeling of monotony, but it will also provide a building block toward jump training in both Open and Utility. It builds the puppy's confidence in jumping and begins to develop the timing and rhythm required for jumping later on.

If you have a set of Broad Jumps, use one turned up on end. You now have an eight-inch height for your dog to jump. The end pieces should be turned away from you.

Secure it so it doesn't topple over and frighten the puppy. If you don't have a set of Broad Jumps, use a board approximately five feet in length and eight inches high. Paint it white. Again, make sure that the board is properly secured.

Place the board in an area where you have approximately ten feet of space on either side of it. Put a lead on and take the puppy to look over the jump. Put your hand on it and tap the board. Let the dog sniff at it. Show that the board is not a threat.

Keep the puppy on your left side. Starting approximately ten feet from the jump, walk the pup at a brisk pace toward the jump. Don't try to make the dog heel. When you are approximately two feet from the board, give the command Over (or Jump, or whatever command you are comfortable with). Adjust your pace so that you can place your right foot approximately six to eight inches from the board, and then, without breaking your stride, *hop* over it with your left foot. As *you* hop over, your puppy will go over with you. Keep the lead loose. As the dog lands, praise enthusiastically.

It helps to practice walking up to the jump *without* the puppy until you are sure of your footing. When you can do it effortlessly, then work with the puppy. Remember, your left leg is the guide leg that the puppy follows.

Once you've jumped over the board with the puppy, don't attempt to jump back the other way, but rather continue around back to where you started. Don't have the dog sit or come to the Heel position. Just let the pup enjoy the jumping experience. Jump your dog no more than three or four times at most during the training session.

There is a common handler problem that arises during this exercise. As the command to jump is given, the handler draws the lead taut. This lifts the pup's front feet off the ground and literally hauls the dog over the board. A smaller dog can be pulled off the ground and propelled through the air this way. This is not jumping. Moreover, you can inadvertently hurt the puppy or make the puppy wary about jumping in the future.

I remember a handler at one of my clinics who told me how much her dog loved to jump and never balked at a jump. She wanted me to see how good the dog was. As I watched her, I realized that every time she got to the jump, she hauled up on the lead and yanked the dog off his feet and over the jump. I had a really hard time convincing her that this is what she was doing.

We finally attached an elastic band between the dog's collar and the snap swivel on the lead. Off they went. She got up to the jump and, as usual, went to pull the dog over. The elastic broke and the dog was left standing there watching her go! If she didn't pull her dog over the jump, the dog didn't go. They weren't beginners. It was in the more advanced stages of training that this was happening. Now that is definitely unintentional training!

Therefore, use your lead correctly and allow enough slack *for the dog to move freely.* As you come close to the jump, make sure you don't pull up on the lead, unbalancing the puppy or pulling the puppy off the ground.

An assortment of toys used during training "playtime." The most important point of this kind of play is to let the puppy win the game.

KPT TRAINING PLAY

When I start talking about playing with your puppy, most dog owners wonder what there is to say. When they play, most of them run around a bit with the puppy, play chase or throw a squeak toy for the puppy to fetch. There is an occasional game of tug-of-war with an old sock or pull toy, and that's it.

I'm not criticizing this kind of playing by any means; it's an important part of every puppy's life. But the type of playing that I want to teach is a method of controlled play that takes advantage of the puppy's curiosity and sense of fun. It uses this enthusiasm to teach *taking and giving back* toys. *This is a building block of great importance.* You add two important words to their vocabulary: Take and Give. They will learn to hold objects in their mouths and also give them back to you. This will stand them in good stead in Open training, when it's time for them to *take* and *give* the dumbbell.

In addition, because the learning process is made enjoyable, they won't have an unreasonable reluctance to working with the dumbbell. Play this way on a fairly frequent basis.

Special Toys

The toys I use and recommend for this type of playtime are "special" toys. My personal assortment includes an old corncob, large and small sponge balls, metal and wooden dowels of assorted sizes (all available at hardware stores), a chew toy shaped like a miniature dumbbell with strips of leather tied on so it can be dangled, even a plastic hot dog. I've got a metal cricket and a little spring jump toy to catch their interest. There are wooden dowels covered with plastic. There are all kinds of ordinary things that make up into a variety of special toys.

The most important point of this playtime is to *let the puppy win*. A puppy who never wins feels like a loser and is going to call it quits on you.

There are no corrections during this playtime either. *It's time for fun*. If you play with a tug toy for instance, let the puppy get it away from you. Let your dog be the winner! If the dog gives back a toy, or runs and fetches a toy and brings it back to you, be enthusiastic and give lots of praise. Your dog will feel like a million-dollar winner!

Most dogs love to carry balls and sticks and toys of all sorts. Start playing with whatever your dog likes best. Have a variety of toys nearby. If one of them doesn't catch the puppy's interest, another one will. I found dangling a chew-toy dowel from a leather thong generally gets attention. I've also found that dowels with balls attached interest puppies.

When you find a dowel that's a comfortable size for your puppy, put a sponge ball on either end of it. When you offer it, make a fist around each of the balls with your knuckles facing the puppy. This guides the pup to take it from the center. Don't move too quickly. The puppy won't be able to follow your hand movement.

Talk to the puppy as you're offering toys. For instance, "Take it. Want it? Take it!" When the puppy takes it, "You've got it. You've got it! Oh, what a g-o-o-o-d dog. Oh, that's a good dog!" Keep the dialogue running as long as it takes for the puppy to take the toy. Once the dog takes it, give lots of praise. However, don't allow the pup to chew on it.

When you're ready to take the toy back, don't yank it out of the dog's mouth. If puppy won't give it up, lightly press the dog's lips against the lower teeth with your thumb and index finger while keeping up your cheerful conversation. *Don't scold*!

If the puppy isn't too keen on the wooden dowel at first, you can

Have a variety of toys. If one doesn't spark any interest, another will. Playing this way sets in place building blocks that teach the puppy to **TAKE** and **GIVE**, preparing for eventual work with the dumbbell.

cover it with clear plastic tubing available at any hardware store. You can do the same thing with a metal dowel to accustom dogs gradually to the feel of metal.

If you throw a toy for your puppy to retrieve, don't throw it too far. And don't correct how your dog brings it back to you. When you throw toys, play in a controlled area where the pup can't run off with them.

Whether you play with the balls on either end of a dowel, or set a spring toy to pop up and catch the dog's attention, make these sessions fun. If your puppy enjoys the game and gets your full approval and attention, he wins! If you laugh with your puppy, if you smile and say how smart he is, your dog wins! If you give your unqualified approval, the pup will always look forward to this special time.

Along with the great pleasure you will get from enjoying the games, *you are setting building blocks in place*. The puppy will respond to you in order to bask in your approval and praise. You will have built a bridge of affection and trust that over time will grow stronger and stronger. I know this sounds a bit flowery, but psychologically speaking it is positive behavior training that works—and besides, it's just plain fun!

Novice Training

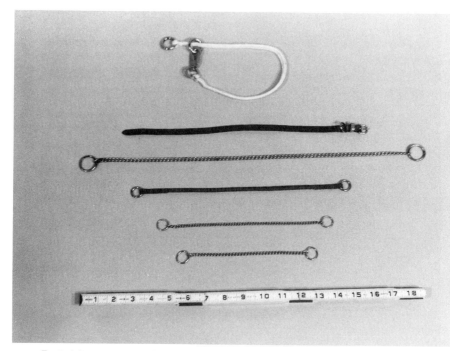

For training, a narrow nylon slip collar is preferable. It should have no more than 2 to 4 inches of extra length when drawn up around the dog's neck. If your dog has a large head, try a snap-around collar (top row). They are not allowed in AKC Obedience competition but are excellent for training.

3

The Basics: Expectations, Equipment and Exercises

FUNDAMENTALS

This chapter presents Novice Obedience training, for those interested in AKC competition as well as for the person who is solely interested in a well-behaved house pet. For the person who is not familiar with AKC competition, the training techniques presented here will give an idea of what is involved. Frequently, as handlers progress, they find the idea of competing at an AKC show appealing and join in this wonderful sport with great enthusiasm.

However, whatever your goal, work your dog with such affection and enthusiasm that it is contagious. That way, your dog will enjoy training as much as you. Such an approach will bring pleasure, satisfaction and success to both your efforts.

PLATEAUS

Most dogs, during the first weeks of training, make impressive, steady progress. This is a wonderful time in which handlers go from believing they can do nothing with their playful puppy, to believing that, with perseverance, *all* is possible. Expectations rise!

Then, for no apparent reason, about the fifth or sixth week of training the dog suddenly appears incapable of grasping the most simple commands. He acts confused, as though trying to understand a language never heard before and perform exercises never seen before. Do not despair. It is only that you have *reached a plateau!*

Take comfort in the fact that you are not alone in this depressing place. This seems to be a natural response on the dog's part to vigorous, repetitive training. Your dog is saying, in his own wonderful way, *enough!*

This is the time to back off on your training a little. Lighten up. Spend time having some fun and give the dog a few days off. During this time reevaluate your training methods. Be sure you are not misusing words when you give commands. Consider whether you have worked beyond the dog's level of concentration. Give yourself time to deal with your frustration.

Then start again with a short period of Heeling and a few Sits. Then stop. Make your daily training period brief and try working on one exercise at a time. Praise as you work. Let your dog know that when he does well, you are *very pleased*. That will help serve as great motivation.

Gradually, go back to your more structured training program. You will find that giving a little "vacation" will bring the dog out of the doldrums and get her back to work far better than increased training sessions and demoralizing corrections.

EQUIPMENT

In Novice training, select lightweight equipment. *Use the lightest possible collar and lead that is appropriate to the size and weight of your dog.* In addition, the equipment must be balanced. The collar, lead and snap swivel on the lead should all be appropriately matched.

Six Months of Age to Adult—Selecting Equipment

When the puppy is over four months old, select a soft, flat, braided, narrow nylon buckle collar for daily use, one-half inch or five-eighths inch wide. For a much larger puppy, there are one-inch collars. This collar can have the usual identification tags and rabies tags attached.

Some owners keep training slip collars on their dogs all the time. This is not my preference. If you do choose to use this type of collar every day, put the tags on a separate snap swivel that can be removed from the collar during training.

For training, I recommend a narrow nylon slip collar with no more than two to three inches of extra length when it is drawn up around the dog's neck. Beginners will not have a fast enough response time on corrections if the collar is too large. Correction is a matter of timing, it should be immediate. *If the slip collar is too long, it makes for ineffective corrections.*

If your dog has a large head, with a lot of furnishings and a narrow neck, try a snap-around nylon slip collar. They are not allowed in the AKC Obedience ring, but are excellent for training use. They don't need to go over the dog's head and ears. You can get a better fit in many cases with a collar that isn't forced over the head. Always remember, *the better the fit, the better your correction control.*

Leads

For your lead, select a one-half-inch to three-quarter-inch cotton web lead with a small snap swivel. I recommend the cotton web lead because it is easy to handle, folds well and doesn't cut into your hands the way a metal link or plastic lead might. Leather leads are available, but I really don't like leather leads for several reasons. Usually, they are fitted with large, heavy snap swivels. They also stretch when they get wet. They're not very easy to fold into your hand as you train either. Plastic, you will find, stiffens when it is cold. If the dog pulls it through your hand, it burns.

The size of your snap swivel must be balanced for the equipment. If you select an appropriate lightweight lead for your dog, and it has a huge snap swivel more suitable for a small pony than for a dog, it isn't balanced. What is the effect? First of all, the heavy snap swivel is like an anchor around the dog's neck. Moreover, when you make a correction using a heavy snap swivel you are telegraphing the correction, minimizing its effectiveness and promoting nagging. The heavy swivel can also hit the dog on the side of the head, causing him to go wide to avoid it.

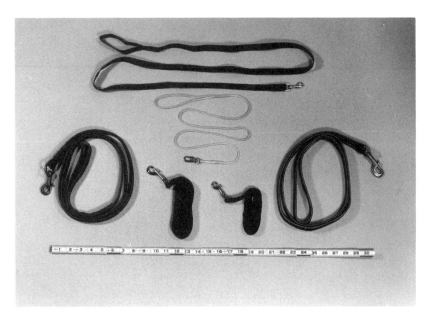

Cotton web leads are preferable because they are easy to handle and fold well into the hand when working.

The snap swivel should be balanced, matching your lead (see upper row). Don't buy leads with either oversized or flimsy snap swivels (as shown in the bottom row).

In dog classes, some inexperienced handlers are afraid the dog will get away from them. These are the people who usually put heavier equipment on their dogs. They decide they are not going to take any chances. If they haven't learned timing and leverage yet and are relying on brute strength to drag the dog around, of course they are going to think that they need heavy equipment. They're yanking and pulling the dog all the time. That's nagging. *That's negative training.* This is a poor way to handle the dog because it gives the wrong idea of what training is suppose to be.

Then, too, there are people in class who are actually afraid of their dogs. These dogs have learned to control the handler. They are usually fitted out in heavy equipment, too. Heavy equipment won't cure that problem. Good training will.

Training Collars

I recommend nylon training collars over steel-link collars. Even the smaller-gauge metal collars are much heavier in weight. Therefore, any corrections given will require a harder pull. In addition, the dog hears the metal collar sliding up as you go to correct. This telegraphs the correction and minimizes its effectiveness. Many trainers, particularly those with larger dogs, tend to favor steel-link collars because they think they're stronger. This is not the case. If you check the test strength of the collars and leads (it is usually given on the brand tags) you find little or no difference in the load strength they can handle. Nylon slip collars are more comfortable for your dog. They don't catch in the fur and pull, nor do they pinch the neck.

The nylon slip collar used during training has two rings. One is stationary at the end of the collar—this is referred to as "live ring." The other ring slides freely along the collar and is called the "dead ring." To put the collar on your dog correctly, hold the *live* ring, that is the one at the end of the collar, in your left hand. The right hand holds the collar about halfway along its length. This creates a shape like the letter *P* turned on its side. While facing the dog, slip the collar over the dog's head and check to be sure that there is no more than two to three inches of extra length when the collar is drawn up around the dog's neck.

It is important that the collar be put on the dog correctly. If you give a correction with the slip collar on incorrectly, it will tighten up and remain tight around the neck. It will not loosen immediately after the correction is given, as it should.

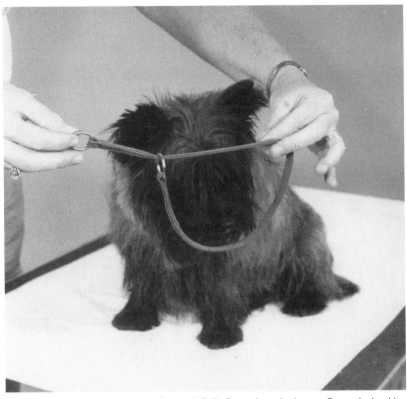

P is the *P*erfect way to *P*ut on a collar, so it *P*ulls *P*roperly and releases *P*romptly. Looking at the picture, the stationary end to the left is the live ring. The ring that slides freely along the collar is the dead ring.

If you use a slip collar with a snap swivel, it is put on in the same way. Face the dog. Hold the *live* ring at the end of the collar in your left hand. Bring the snap swivel around and under the dog's chin and attach it to the free sliding ring. Again, keep in mind the *P* shape. This type of collar can be used in training sessions, but is not allowed in AKC competition.

Use the training collar *only during training sessions*. For everyday, use a flat nylon buckle collar with ID and other tags attached.

Frequently I am asked about spiked collars for training. I *never* like to see a spiked collar used to train a dog. I don't allow them in any of our training classes. There are better ways to train a dog than to use such equipment.

There are areas of the country, however, where they are very popular. People are told by some that it cuts down on corrections

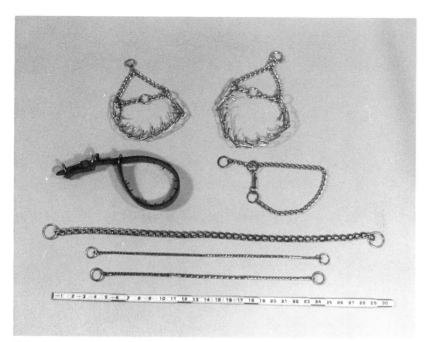

Spiked collars, although popular in some areas of the country, are not allowed in any of my classes. I believe there is no place for these collars in dog training.

because one sharp correction with a spike collar is more effective than a lot of little corrections with a nylon collar. I don't agree. If you correct *properly* with a soft nylon collar, you won't need a lot of little corrections and you will get excellent results. I see no advantage to spike collars. I don't believe they promote the proper motivation for your dog to work well for you, and they have been known to damage vocal cords.

HOLDING THE LEAD

Two Hands

Although we described how to hold the lead in KPT, its important enough to review it here. How you hold the lead will make a difference in how well your dog will begin Heeling on-lead. You should have your lead under total control for best results.

I prefer that beginning trainers hang the loop of the lead over the right thumb. Holding the loop, raise your right hand to waist height.

When you begin training, hold the lead in both hands for better control. The left hand gives the dog guidance and correction.

Slide the left hand down about three feet. Fold that amount in several folds across the right palm. The right hand, holding the folds, continues to be held at waist level. The left hand holds the lead loosely at the left side below the waist. The snap swivel should be hanging downward. The dog should feel no pressure on her neck. Holding the lead in this way gives you good control. The left hand can give the dog guidance and correction.

Left Hand Only

As you become more experienced, you may prefer to hold the lead in the left hand only. The lead is folded and held at the side. Allow sufficient lead so that the snap swivel attached to the collar hangs downward. Corrections when holding the lead in the left hand are made by holding the left arm close to your side and twisting the wrist.

As you become experienced, choose the method that works for you. As a beginner, however, I recommend that you hold the lead in both hands.

Right Hand Only

Some handlers are taught to hold the lead in the right hand. The lead is folded and held in the right palm at waist level. Sufficient lead is allowed so that the snap swivel hangs down. Corrections are given by a sharp tug. Depending upon the size of the dog and/or how difficult, two hands may be required to give the corrections. When heeling with the lead in the right hand only, the left arm should swing naturally.

One of the disadvantages of holding the lead in the right hand is that when trying to give corrections, you can pull the dog against your leg, unintentionally training her to crowd. I do not recommend that beginning trainers hold the lead in the right hand only. It doesn't give the inexperienced handler sufficient control.

NOVICE—BASIC EXERCISES

These are important exercises for your dog to know before you begin your heeling exercises. They consist of the Stand, Sit and Down commands and the hand signals for Stay and Down.

Even if you have taken your puppy through these exercises in

KPT, I recommend that you repeat the exercises at this point as a reinforcement. Remember, these exercises are building blocks that fit into more advanced levels of training. Be sure your dog learns them thoroughly.

Encourage and praise your dog when he does well. Be sure to listen to the sound of your own voice. When the dog needs correction, add an authoritative sound to your voice, not an angry or harsh tone.

Novice Stand

Kneel with the dog in front of you, the head toward your right hand. With your right hand, knuckles pointing into the neck, take hold of the collar behind the dog's head. This controls the dog's head. With the edge of your left hand, fingers together and palm down, touch the upper part of the inside of the dog's rear leg. The back of your hand should barely be brushing the dog's underside. This keeps your dog in place as you pull up and toward lightly on the collar with your right

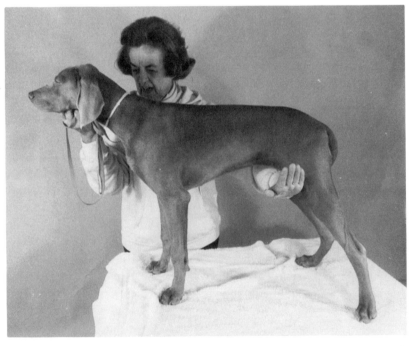

If it is more comfortable for you, even if your 6-month-old puppy is large, you can teach the basic exercises on a sturdy table with a nonskid top.

hand. Keep the pressure of each hand movement about equal. Don't pull up so hard that your dog's feet leave the floor. As you do these two movements, give the command. Use the dog's name first, then say "S-t-a-n-d" in a drawn-out voice. Be sure the dog is standing comfortably. When she is steady, let go of the collar and, using your right hand, give the Stay hand signal as you say "S-t-a-y," this command drawn out also.

To give the Stay hand signal, place your right hand in front of the dog's face. Keep your fingers together, hand firm, palm toward the dog. Give a sweeping movement toward his face. Move slowly so he can follow your hand. Stop a few inches in front of the dog's face. Be sure the movement is not aggressive or menacing. Repeat the Stay command until you are able to remove your left hand from the front of the dog's hind legs and have him remain standing in place. Don't forget lots of praise when your dog is doing well!

Be sure the commands are given in a cheerful voice, with each command drawn out like a stretched rubber band. Never forget to praise your dog when you are done with an exercise.

Have the dog on lead while teaching the Stand if it gives you a better sense of control. Lay it out in front of the dog so that it is available if the dog starts to move away.

Novice Sit

This exercise can be done immediately following the Stand. Continue to kneel on the side of your dog in a comfortable position. Remember not to hover. Stand your dog facing toward your right hand. Take hold of the back of the dog's collar in your right hand, knuckles pointing into the neck. Then, with your left hand, fingers together, palm down, gently push in at the back of the dog's knees, on the hamstrings above the hocks, so that her legs fold into a sit. At the same time, with the right hand, pull slightly up and back on the collar. Use the dog's name and give the command Sit as you do these two movements. Switch the collar from the right hand to the left hand. With the right hand, give the Stay command. Keep your movements smooth, slow and gentle and your voice sounding pleased. When your dog sits steadily, be sure to praise with enthusiasm.

These two exercises can be practiced one after the other until you need only the pressure of your right hand on the collar to have the dog respond to the commands.

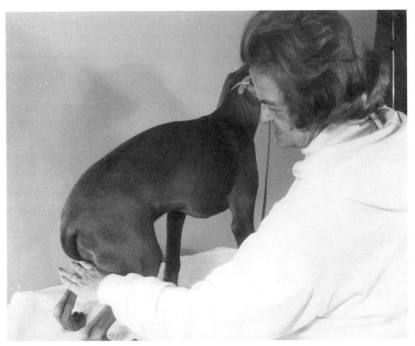

To teach the Sit, pull up slightly on the collar while gently pushing in at the back of the dog's legs above the hock.

Novice Down

This exercise may take a little more patience since dogs do not like to feel off-balance. If you try to keep the legs as relaxed as possible when you lift them and speak quietly and encouragingly, it will make your job easier.

Kneel on your right knee. Keep your left knee up to form an L in which the dog sits, facing toward your right hand. The inside of your left foot should be directly behind the dog. Hold the collar in your right hand. Reach your left arm over your dog's back and raise his left leg up a few inches. Shake it gently to relax it and put it back down.

Reassure your dog by saying what a good dog she is. Then switch the collar to your left hand and pick up her right leg in your right hand, shake it gently and put it back down on the floor. Do this a few times to relax the dog. Praise her for letting you lift her legs. Keep talking in an encouraging way. Then raise both legs up together, say the dog's name and give the Down command in a drawn-out voice. Keep rocking

Dogs do not like to feel off-balance. Teaching the Down takes patience. Whether you work on a nonskid table or the floor depends on your agility. In either case reassure the dog by shaking first one leg, then the other. Finally, shaking both legs, pull them gently forward and completely lower the dog. Keep your hand on the dog's back initially to keep your pup relaxed.

41

If you work on the floor, place your left foot behind the dog's rump to keep him in place. The pup's head faces toward your right. If you teach the basic exercises on the floor, do not hover over the dog.

the legs to keep them relaxed as you stretch them out and down in front of the dog. Once he is down, put your left hand lightly on your dog's back to keep him in place. With your right hand, give a Stay command and hand signal. As the dog lays quietly, say how pleased you are with him. If necessary, keep repeating the Stay command until your dog is steady.

If your dog does not stay down, or resists going down altogether, keep your voice calm, but add a note of authority to the commands. This does not mean that you should sound angry. That will only make him more anxious and determined to get up. Simply sound calm, but firm.

When you praise on this exercise, be a little careful not to sound so enthusiastic that your dog is encouraged to leap up.

This exercise should be done with the lead on the collar but just laying in front of the dog. This gives an added feeling of control to the handler.

After the dog understands the Down command and begins re-sponding when given the command, reinforce it with a Down hand signal. To give this hand signal you raise your right arm at the elbow, fingers together, with your palm facing forward. You then bring your hand down, past the dog's face, in a smooth motion. Move slowly at first, so the dog can follow the movement.

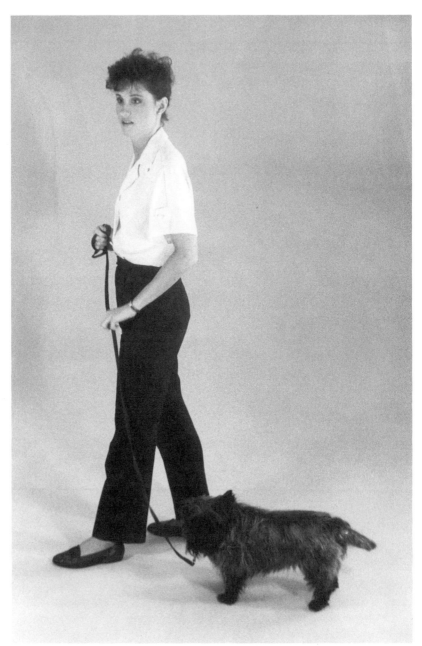

Lagging is a common problem. Pick up your pace. Brisk Heeling keeps the dog's attention.

4

Heeling On-Lead

T O BEGIN Heeling on-lead, the dog wears a soft training collar, either a slip collar or one with a snap swivel. There should be no more than two to three inches of extra length when it is drawn up around the dog's neck.

Attach the lead to the dead ring of the training collar—not to the ring at the end of the collar. When you are teaching a new exercise, never give a strong correction. If the dog is learning and does not know what to do, it does not make sense to give a correction. Appropriate corrections may come later, but only when the dog knows what is expected.

Position the dog at your left side, in line with your leg. The dog should be sitting close to you, but not touching you, and should be sitting straight.

The lead is held, folded, in your right hand at waist level, hanging downward from the dog's collar. Your left hand is down at your side, relaxed, loosely holding the lead, but ready to grasp it and give a light, quick twist of the wrist to forestall a mistake or issue a correction.

As you move off, use the dog's name and give the Heel command. Step off on your left foot. Starting on the left foot gives your dog the cue to move with you.

Keep in mind that initially the dog is *not ready* and does not know what you are going to do. It is your job to communicate with her.

When you say your dog's name, you capture her attention. Pause a second. In that second your dog becomes alert, listening for what is coming next: "Heel!" She now knows what you want, but needs time, however, to do it. When she hears the command, she is sitting, and needs time to get her whole body up and to start moving her legs. With very small dogs, this is a quick movement, but with the larger dog, it takes more time. Remember this before you start to move. When you step out on your left foot, make it a *half step*. Don't try for a giant step that gets you moving quickly. Don't even try for a normal step. Start with a simple half step. You will be giving your dog time to get up and get moving. At this point, you must encourage. *Do not correct!* *Sound enthusiastic.*

The lead will tighten as you move forward and give a light tug forward. You don't want to unintentionally leave your dog behind on the very first step, a very bad habit to allow to develop. If you do it in the Obedience ring, it can cost a half point or more. Use words to move her along with you, words like "Let's go—good dog!" Keep the voice pleasant and light. *How you use your voice when you are training is very important.*

HOW TO MOVE WITH YOUR DOG

After the initial half step, walk at a normal pace. If you continue to take small steps, you encourage lagging when the dog comes to realize you are accommodating her. Move naturally. It is important to keep your feet straight and low to the ground as you move forward. Moving your feet this way helps the dog heel properly. Remember the dog's point of view down there.

It takes two to Heel. Don't expect the dog to do everything. While it is important that the dog should learn to adjust to your movements, it is also important to give movements that help your dog perform the exercise well. Don't give the added burden of having to dodge awkward mannerisms and clumsy feet.

It's helpful to practice alone in front of a long mirror for a bit before Heeling with your dog. If you try it, you may be dismayed at first to see how you walk. Work at walking in a straight line and keep your feet low. Select a point in front of you and aim for it. This will keep you from veering off on a tangent. Move at a normal pace. Don't get in the habit of moving too quickly. When you hurry, you miss what is happening. You need to be in control and aware of what

46

your dog is doing. The more you practice, the smoother will be your movements. You will be better able to work with your dog.

YOUR POSTURE

As you work, keep your head up and your body straight. Don't look sloppy. However, a ramrod, pseudo-military posture isn't correct either. You want to maintain an upright relaxed stance.

If you must bend to the dog for any reason, to praise for instance, bend from the knees. Never hang over the dog or manage to twist yourself around like a corkscrew. This puts you in an awkward, unbalanced position. You can't come up smoothly and quickly to a straight position. Also, many dogs really dislike being hovered over.

If you give the dog a crooked body to line up on, you cannot expect her to stand straight or sit straight alongside. I cannot emphasize this point strongly enough. *Give the dog a straight body to line up with.* You are the point of reference as she works.

THE AUTOMATIC SIT

Once you have begun training in Heeling exercises, your dog will be taught to sit each time you halt. It may be necessary, when you begin, to stoop next to your dog and assist her into a correct sit position.

You can use the Sit command the first few times if necessary. Try to eliminate the command as soon as possible, so that the dog will learn to sit automatically. Be sure that, right from the start, the dog sits correctly. Don't be satisfied with sloppy sits. If necessary, use your lead and give short, smart snaps to get the dog to sit correctly. Be consistent, and your dog will soon learn to sit automatically when you halt in heeling. Be sure to praise when she does well.

Your footwork is important in Heeling. When you come to a halt, bring your left foot up and place it down last. This will become an additional cue to the dog to sit. Once your dog gets used to this, don't make it obvious; make the step a natural movement.

If you are in a ring at a show and the judge says "Halt," you are not required to stop instantly. You're allowed to take an extra step or two, if necessary, to get the left foot in place last. Place your left foot down in a normal manner. If you kick your heel or thump your foot, it will be considered a second command to the dog, resulting in a zero score.

TALK TO YOUR DOG

Once again, as you train your dog it is important to talk in an encouraging way. It is equally important that you speak pleasantly and in a natural voice. I suggest you *tape a practice training session and listen* to yourself. This is an excellent way to hear yourself as your dog hears you. It will enable you to evaluate the tone of voice you use. It will also give you an idea of how *much* you talk to your dog while training. You'll be able to judge whether what you say and how you say it is encouraging or discouraging. You will also be able to hear whether you are talking too much or too little.

Remember, when you say your dog's name, make it sound happy. Make it sound like something good.

When you give a command to the dog, give it in a clear, *pleasant*, firm voice: "Heel!" Don't start out sounding as though you are declaring war on the dog. You may be the one to lose.

Believe that both of you are engaged in a mutual learning experience that is enjoyable to both. The expectation (good or bad) in your voice will set the tone of the training session.

As you Heel with the dog, talk with lots of enthusiasm. "Good girl!" "That's a good dog!" "That's it. That's it." "Move along, now!" "What a good dog!" *Never* sound as if you are pleading or coaxing.

On the other hand, you do not want to sound angry or anxious either. Keep your voice encouraging and cheerful. If you feel self-conscious about talking to your dog as you work, you are not alone. I've had thirty or forty people heeling their dogs around the ring and I've had to compliment them on what a quiet group they were. Remember, silence or diffidence will lose the dog's attention.

If you must make a correction while Heeling, don't nag. Nagging will only cause the dog to turn off eventually. Give one firm correction and return to an encouraging attitude and praise.

A word of caution about the phrases you use when talking to your dog outside of training. Have appropriate phrases ready that will not confuse the dog. Use them frequently. Training commands include the words "Come," "Down," "Stay" and "Sit." A good phrase to use when you want to encourage your dog might be "Let's go," rather than "Come on," "No jump" is a better choice than "Get down." You avoid confusing the dog by using these phrases rather than training words.

TAKE SUFFICIENT TIME

It is important for handlers to approach dog training in a calm and controlled manner. Your dog will not be under control if *you* are not under control. Excitability and anger produce resentful, poorly trained dogs.

It is also important not to feel hurried as you work. Be sure the amount of time you allow for each training session is long enough to work in a calm, alert way. Train in a relaxed and easy manner. Concentrate fully on what you are doing. Observe carefully what your dog is doing. With this approach you will develop the concentration necessary to be alert to your dog's behavior cues, and be able to "read" her accurately. This is extremely important. It will help you catch errors before they creep into the dog's performance and prevent unintentional training.

Have the words you want to use ready. You will then be prepared to react in the *correct* way. You want, if at all possible, to be able to *forestall mistakes before the dog actually makes the error*, not correct them afterward. *Prevention is better than correction.*

We all know how time consuming correcting problems becomes and how much patience and energy is required to weed them out. I would like to discuss some additional ways hurried lessons can adversely affect the dog's performance.

If, for instance, you are heeling the dog and you halt only a second or two here and a second or two there, and then you're impatiently off and running again because you are in a hurry, you will wind up with sloppy sits. In addition, the dog will be on edge and begin to anticipate commands. She may even start forging out in front of you. You are unintentionally training all kinds of errors into the dog's performance, errors that are caused by hurrying.

If you have allowed yourself a sufficient amount of time for your training session but still find that you hurry through the exercises, I suggest *counting*. It is an excellent method to use to slow down. Whatever you are doing, *count it out*. As you step out in Heeling, for example, count to yourself. This will help you stay low-keyed. When you halt, count to ten before moving along. Doing this will definitely help you keep in control. It is one way to be sure that the *dog is heeling for you*. Don't you start heeling for the dog. Don't let her be the one to set the pace. I have seen it happen both with beginners and experienced handlers.

The dog starts heeling faster and faster, and pretty soon she's leading the handler around completely. It's unintentional training. Usually it doesn't enter the handler's mind that the dog is not following. In fact, the handler frequently decides that he or she has a really alert heeling dog. Remember, the purpose of Heeling, or any training exercise, is for the dog to adapt to you.

This is not to say that you should not Heel frequently at the stride that is natural to the dog. You are working as a team and you want to bring out the best in her. However, *you* choose the stride and *you* change the stride, and the dog must learn to adapt to your choices.

THE DOG'S NATURAL STRIDE

With each dog there is a certain gait that seems natural and right for that specific animal. The dog gets a little lilt in her stride and moves along as though really alert and interested. Your dog will be alert and interested, too, if *you* find her pace and use it. Use the dog's *natural* stride. Work just fast enough so that she can't pay attention to other things. At that special pace, she looks good and feels good. You'll know that stride when you hit it just by observing the way your dog comes to life.

KEEPING THE DOG'S ATTENTION AS YOU HEEL

When heeling, change direction frequently. Don't get in the habit of Heeling in one direction for too long a time. You will lose the dog's attention. She already knows how to walk, and without any challenges given enough time, she will become inattentive. Lagging, forging and wide heeling are often caused by the loss of the dog's attention.

It is equally important to keep the Heeling patterns interesting. If you tend to habitually follow the same Heeling patterns, the dog is going to become bored and Heel poorly.

Keep the dog alert when training by whistling, talking or whatever it takes to keep the dog's attention. And watch how you use your guide leg. Hold your body well, because as the dog gets used to working with you, she'll take cues from your posture and movements. Don't give mixed signals to the dog. In addition, your voice should be friendly and relaxed. The command voice should have more authority but still sound calm and in control. Have the lead under control. Don't say one thing to the dog with your voice and another thing with the lead.

Prepare before each training session. Know what you are going to do. Have your training words ready for success or correction!

SLOW AND FAST HEELING

The point of the slow and fast Heeling exercise is to demonstrate that your dog is capable of Heeling in a controlled manner and changing pace. If your dog moves too quickly and does not adjust to your slower movement, use slow Heeling as a correction. That may seem very obvious, but you would be amazed at how few people put that concept into practice. Many handlers change *their* speed instead, just to keep up with the dog. Slow down and let the dog adjust to you.

As you change your pace to slow Heeling, don't go into a pitty-pat mincing step. Keep the size of your step normal and slow down gradually. Don't try to slow down instantly. There is a lapse of a few seconds as you move into slow Heeling or out of it when you return to normal Heeling. You should appear to float into and out of the pace gradually and smoothly, allowing the dog to stay with you.

Fast Heeling is done in the same way. It can't be "instant fast." You must move in a controlled manner. Fast Heeling can best be described as a little trot with your feet close to the ground. You don't run in place. You move into it gradually, you return to normal gradually. I have found it helps to work a little faster in training so you can drop back a bit and move at an easy pace in the show ring.

KEEP THE DOG THINKING

An excellent exercise to work on while Heeling is to do an about-turn and immediately change your pace to fast. Get your dog used to a variety of exercises in different sequences. Keep the dog thinking. Consistently doing the routines exactly as they are called for in the Obedience ring makes for bored, mechanical dogs. There are dogs working in Utility that become completely confused if their exercises are out of sequence. You don't want a dog of that caliber. Dogs must be kept alert, thinking about what they are doing. Remember that dogs who give mechanical performances are in trouble if they have to stop and think. Always work your dog so that she responds to the *situation*. A dog lives most of life outside the show ring. Your training should carry over into everyday life. *Because a dog can move diligently through the exercises in the ring, this doesn't necessarily mean the dog is well trained.*

A well-trained dog should behave well at home, at class, in fact anywhere you both go, and be acceptable to neighbors. In order to accomplish this, you must hold her attention when training and keep your dog alert by varying the exercise routines sufficiently to be assured she is thinking and responsive. By approaching training in this way you will have well-rounded dogs—not strictly show-oriented or mechanical performers.

FORGING

Should your dog begin forging when Heeling on-lead, bring the lead around behind you, holding it in the right hand with sufficient tension so that the dog cannot pull out ahead of you. Once your dog is back in position, loosen up on the lead and do a left turn.

Begin to make the turn once you have the dog in the correct position beside you. Keep Heeling forward, if necessary, until you have her in place. Should you have more of a problem getting the dog back beside you, try taking hold of the lead in your left hand, and pull straight back on the lead to give a correction.

Once the dog is back in position, say her name and give the Heel command. Then, make your left turn by stepping across the dog with the right leg. *Do not hit into her with your left leg.* That is not a good correction for this problem. Making the left turn keeps the the dog at your side and prevents forging.

LAGGING

A great many lagging problems are caused by sloppy, inattentive walking on the handler's part. To correct lagging, get a little lilt to your walk. There is a certain speed at which the dog looks good and feels good. There is some spring as she moves along. Don't Heel in a lackadaisical manner. You want the dog to *come to life!* So, pick up your tempo. A brisk Heeling speed helps hold attention. Your dog won't have time *not* to pay attention.

It helps, too, if you don't walk forward too long. Do About Turns. Circle left and right. It isn't easy to keep this up for any length of time, especially if you have a large breed of dog, so get in shape!

CROWDING

There are several training errors that encourage crowding. Some handlers work the lead too tightly, pulling the dog toward them. Be sure, when you are Heeling, that the lead has enough slack so that the snap swivel is hanging downward.

The handler who praises a dog by pulling her close to the leg is unintentionally teaching the dog to crowd. Praise the larger breeds by rubbing the dog's chin lightly. You can also scratch the dog's neck on the *right* side. If you do this, you teach that if she keeps her head straight, she'll get petted. If not, no pets! You do the same thing with smaller dogs except you've got a bit more of a job getting down to their level. Petting or scratching the right shoulder will keep your dog from leaning into you.

At home, when your dog comes to you for petting, don't pull her against your legs or you'll find this will carry over into training class. Your dog enjoys the affection and will want to be close to you. So be alert, and avoid this kind of unintentional training.

If your dog Heels wide, use a curb to practice. It can also be used to correct crooked Sits.

You can also work on top of the curb, along the edge.

Whatever the reason for your dog's crowding problem, it is important that you do not correct it in a way that creates resentment.

HEELING WIDE

A simple but effective training aid you can use if the dog tends to heel wide is to use a curb to practice. Walk, with the dog on your left side, between you and the curb.

Don't crowd or bump the dog; let the curb serve as a guide to your dog. When you Heel, keep the dog moving at a brisk pace. (You will both learn to Heel in a straight line.)

It is also a good place to practice Sits if you have a problem with them. It is hard for the dog to sit crooked if the curb is there to keep a straight line.

You can also work on top of the curb. Work with the dog on the outside, along the edge. If she heels or sits wide, she'll fall off. This will be sufficient incentive to keep your dog in the proper Heel position.

These training aids are simple and work well. However, like any training aid, use it only as long as you need it and then eliminate its use. If overused, you can create other problems.

RIGHT AND LEFT TURNS

As you turn with your dog, remember that *your left leg is the dog's guide*. You must use it to relay information. Don't forget, however, the rest of your body is important, too! Keep your head up, body straight, your knees close together and your feet low to the ground. When turning, turn your shoulders and entire body together. Don't twist around from the hip or dip your shoulders. Don't step in front and block the dog's movement.

The footwork is simple. To turn to the left, step out on the left foot, then cross over with your right foot as you pivot. Make it a normal-size step forward. Don't put your right foot down next to the

RIGHT AND LEFT TURN

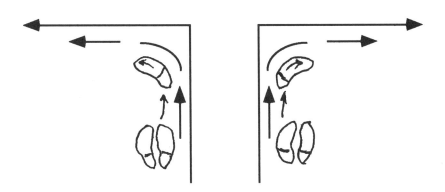

SQUARE -- NOT A CIRCLE

Practice Right and Left Turns without the dog until you can move and pivot smoothly. As your turns improve, gradually develop square turns.

left one on the pivot and do a little two-step. The correct way is to pivot on the left foot and then swing your right foot around and forward into a smooth normal step.

To turn to the right, you follow the same pattern, but in reverse. Step out on the right foot, then cross over with your left foot as you pivot. Bring your left foot around and forward into a normal-size step.

All of us want squared-off turns the first time we try. Initially, I have found that a gradual bend works much better. As your turns improve, gradually develop square turns. Don't be abrupt with the turn, and whatever you do, don't adopt militaristic-looking movements. Most judges don't like to see this in the ring.

Again, I suggest practicing without the dog until you can move and pivot smoothly. The first few times you try it, you may find it a little awkward to keep your balance. We tend to avoid movement on one foot. Some people feel more comfortable on two feet while turning. However, if you get both feet pitter-pattering together on the pivot, it's awkward figuring out which foot to move next after you turn your body. If you're confused at that point, the dog will be, too! So, *initially practice without the dog*!

Never use your leg to push the dog out of the way when you are practicing Left Turns. The dog should come to know the left leg as a guide leg, not as a source of corrections. If a correction is needed on a Left Turn, use the lead (which is in your left hand) to draw the dog back and out of the way.

CIRCLE RIGHT, CIRCLE LEFT

Circling to the right and to the left is an excellent training exercise. It prepares you and your dog for the Figure Eight exercise.

For this exercise, you don't want to walk in a straight line. Start Heeling to your right in a circle that will be approximately four feet wide. Go around the circle once, returning to where you began. You can then continue Heeling in a straight line.

You will have to work to keep the dog in the correct Heel position as you turn right. To do this, drop your right hip back and drop your right shoulder slightly, without twisting your body. The dog will use your body movement as a point of reference while moving around the circle. However, do not move your left arm forward when you are going to make a right turn.

Since the dog is on the outside of the turn, she is going to have to speed up to keep up with you. If *you* move a little more quickly, you will find it encourages the dog to move faster as well. Talking to your dog as you circle will help to keep attention focused on you.

Circling to the left is done in a similar manner. This time you drop your left hip back and drop left shoulder slightly—also without twisting your body. And remember, do not get in the habit of pulling your left arm back when you go to make a left turn.

The dog is on the inside of the circle and must slow down while you maintain your normal speed. Don't let the dog forge ahead. Use the forging corrections, if necessary. Also, talking while circling will help keep your dog at your side.

ABOUT-TURNS

About-turns seem to give a lot of people trouble. This is partially caused by the fact that there are no hard-and-fast rules about how to turn. Your footwork is pretty much of your own choosing. Whatever you do is acceptable as long as it looks normal and natural.

Here, too, initially you want to work on the About-Turn without your dog. Watch how you use your body and your feet. Observing yourself in a mirror would be of great value. It has been my experience that people do not realize how they walk. When they're nervous or anxious in class or in the ring, they are really oblivious. Frequently they don't know left from right! That's why it is very important to practice your movements correctly until they become second nature.

If you have trouble walking in a straight line, as most people do, line up on something. Practice the About-Turn near a wall or along a curb. In that way, if you don't keep your feet straight and turn correctly, you'll know it. Try constantly to be aware of your physical movements. They are one of the dog's most valuable guides if properly executed. *Poor body movement*, on the other hand, *confuses the dog*.

Here are some helpful guidelines if you are not satisfied with your About-Turns. Turn your whole body—shoulders, hips, the entire body—at once. Keep in mind that your left leg is the dog's guide, so learn to use it well. Keep your knees together and your feet straight and low to the ground as you move. If you don't keep your knees together as you turn, your left leg will end up too far behind you when you complete your turn. You may then find yourself two steps ahead of the dog. She's not going to cross over your leg or get tripped up on it. And, if you lift your foot while your leg is back there, you may kick your dog. So keep your knees together and your feet low to the ground. Don't bring your left foot up high, and don't throw it out to

When you do the About Turn, if you drop your left leg too far back as you turn, your leg prevents the dog from moving into the Heel position and causes lagging.

the back or side and force the dog to lag or heel wide to avoid your feet.

Another suggestion that you will find helpful is to make your first step, after you have turned around, a half step. This gives the dog time to move around you and keep up with you and so avoids a lagging problem.

LAGGING ON ABOUT-TURNS

If the dog is lagging, give a Heel command just *before* you do an About-Turn. Give a snap of your lead, use the dog's name and say "Heel!" Then do the About-Turn. In order to get your dog's attention, the command must be given before the turn. Do not let the dog get out of position. If she lags and you find it necessary to keep moving more quickly after the turn, give a correction there also. But remember to make your initial correction before the turn. Don't get into the habit of nagging. A few words of encouragement following the corrections will make for a more enthusiastic feeling and keep her right up there beside you.

ABOUT-TURN AND HALT

When given the command About-Turn and Halt, it can really throw you if you're not prepared.

When you're in the Obedience ring and the judge says "About-Turn and Halt," what does that mean? It means turn around and halt in a reasonable amount of time. It does not mean turn and stop on a dime.

When the judge gives the commands, do your About-Turn movement smoothly. Next, take a step or two, however many it takes to put the right foot down and bring the left up. Slow down and put the left foot down naturally. Don't slap the foot down or click your heels. Of course, the same footwork applies to the Halt without the turn.

Whatever you do, don't straighten up your lead as you halt or add any other little movement. That usually constitutes an extra command. As we all know, an extra command in the show ring could give a zero score.

Many people unintentionally train their dogs to respond only when two commands have been given. They give the verbal command and a subtle secondary command, such as a tug on the lead, a stamping of the foot, a dip of the shoulder or even a very small hand movement. Don't allow yourself to get into these bad training habits.

You will have given the dog sufficient guidance simply by halting consistently on the same foot. *The best cue you can give is to bring the left foot into place last, as previously described.*

If you use this method consistently from the start, the dog will not have to guess whether or not you are actually going to stop. This avoids the problem of slow Sits, backing into a Sit or forging ahead.

CORRECT SITS

How the dog sits presents a varied assortment of problems. Not all of the errors are dog errors, either. Handlers have to take their share of the blame for poor Sits.

There are handlers who step *into* their dog when they halt. This is a very common problem. Is it helping the dog? The handlers think so or they wouldn't have started doing it.

Most handlers who do this are totally unaware that they are accommodating the dog in this way. It becomes such a habit that unless they look carefully at what they are doing, or have someone watch them and correct them, they scarcely believe that they are guilty of this particular error.

If you want to give yourself a little test, try this. Before you halt, pick out a spot ahead of you, walk to the spot and halt *right on that spot*. If you feel off-balance, chances are you are accommodating the dog. Use the curb to correct wide Sits. Walk along the edge of a curb with the dog on the outside. If your dog sits wide, she'll be off the curb.

Do not step into your dog! If *you* are going to move over, why should *she* worry about staying next to you? And if you start stepping into the dog in one area of training, she is likely to let you move into her everywhere else as well.

When you are showing the dog in Obedience, the judge does not give you credit for any Sit where you move into the dog. You can see how important correct Sits are when you realize that you can lose three to five points on Sits alone as you go through your exercises in the show ring!

There is another problem caused by the handler, yet blamed on the dog. That is the dog who sits too far back. When you stop, do not drop your hip back. The dog will misunderstand this body movement and think you are about to do a Left Turn. Practice alone without the dog. If you drop your hip back, see how naturally a Left Turn would seem to follow the movement.

It is imperative that you pay attention to how you move your body. Avoid such habitual errors. Make it your business to know what you are doing so that your dog can take proper cues from you and know the right thing to do.

As you train, expect the dog to sit immediately when you halt. Do not wait for the dog to make up *her* mind when or where to sit. *Give one command, and then enforce it with the lead. As soon as your dog sits, start heeling again.* The second time you stop, you should have the dog's attention. Just give a voice correction this time, but be ready to give a correction with the lead if it proves necessary.

Another training technique that is helpful when the dog sits forward of the handler is to put the lead around behind you. Hold the lead in the right hand as usual. If you have a small dog, hold the lead low. For a larger dog raise your arm higher. In this way you get better leverage. You then have the dog heel and halt alongside of you in the normal fashion. But when you stop, the lead, if it is around behind you, will keep your dog back in proper position until the habit is broken.

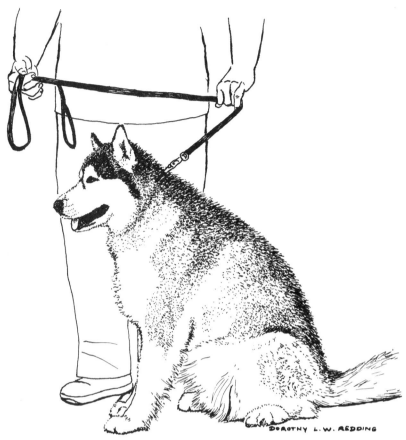

To correct slow Sits, hold the folded lead in your right hand and slide the left hand along it. This hand movement gives the lead a firm backward snap. The lead should be at the back of the dog's head. Do not pull up or forward for this correction.

For the leaning dog, remember to praise correctly and not pull the dog into your legs. If, at any point your dog starts to lean, a good solution is to do a series of Heeling and Halts, but never let her sit long enough to have time to lean in. She'll stop leaning simply by not having the time to do it.

Leaning can also be caused when you give a correction for the Sit. Don't pull on the lead with the right hand to give this correction. If you do, the dog's head will be pulled across in front of your legs and she will be unable to sit straight.

To give a Sit correction, don't pull the lead straight out in front of the dog with your left hand to make a correction either. You can't expect the dog to be able to stretch her neck out with the lead and still get her bottom down on the ground. *The dog will sit crooked if corrected in this manner.* Be sure you give enough lead to enable your dog to sit beside you comfortably with her shoulder at your knee, or for a smaller dog, in line with your ankle. Do not have the lead too slack or you won't be able to get in a fast correction, should it be called for.

If a correction is in order, hold your folded lead firmly in your right hand at waist level. No higher. Then, slide the left hand quickly down the lead. Don't grab at it, just slide the left hand quickly along the lead until it stops behind the dog's neck. *Your hand does not hit the neck.* It stops behind it. This hand movement gives the lead a firm snap. This is the proper way to correct with the lead for the Sit exercise. *Don't pull the lead up or forward.*

Be sure that your dog sits straight right from the start. Don't tolerate crooked Sits at the beginning of your training program thinking that you can refine them later. Heeling and sitting are integrated exercises. You don't want the dog to get in the habit of Heeling well but sitting in a sloppy manner any more than you would tolerate sloppy Heeling and straight Sits. Don't let these two exercises separate in your mind or the dog's mind. It is always easier in the long run to do the exercises correctly from the beginning rather than trying to change bad habits later.

THE FIGURE-EIGHT EXERCISE

The Figure Eight hones Heeling skills by keeping the dog attentive to changes in the handler's tempo and direction of movement. It involves slow, fast and normal Heeling as well as automatic Sits.

When you practice, begin teaching this exercise using two barrels or trash cans as posts if two people are not available to work with you. If you do have two people stand as your posts, they should stand facing each other, eight feet apart. They remain immobile, with their hands folded at waist height for the length of the exercise.

Put the dog on-lead at the Heel position and stand a half step off the midline of the barrels. Using the dog's name, give him the command to Heel and take a half step forward with your left foot. This allows your dog time to get up and begin moving with you before you start into your first turn.

If you decide to take the left turn first, drop your left hip back and drop your shoulder slightly, without twisting your body, so that

FIGURE EIGHT

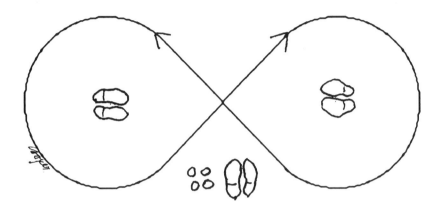

the dog has a straight target to follow. Since this is an inside turn (meaning that the dog is between you and the post), she must learn to slow down in order to stay at the Heel position.

During early practice, slow down on this turn so that the dog gets the idea that *she must slow down*. Eventually she will know to slow down even though you maintain your normal speed.

Be sure to make your turn wide enough as you come around the post so that the dog will not hit into it. Come around the post as if you were doing a circle exercise. Don't make it a narrow oval. Make the turn as *round* as you can. It shouldn't look like you're making a left turn.

As you come around the first post, start making a circle to the right. Drop your right hip back and drop your shoulder slightly, again without twisting your body. This is an outside turn (i.e, the dog is on the outside of you and the post) so she must learn to speed up to keep up with you. Again, during the early stages of training, speed up on the right turn to encourage the dog to move faster.

While doing this exercise, remember to keep your feet low to the ground. Hold the lead properly. Talk to your dog to encourage staying in the Heel position. If the dog forges ahead on the outside turn, give a lead correction to pull her back. If your dog lags on the inside turn,

Make your turns round, not oval, as you practice the Figure Eight. Give yourself enough room to circle without getting too close to the posts.

When you circle right, the dog is on the outside and must move faster to keep up with you. As you come through the center, be attentive to the dog's position. Correct lagging before you start circling around the post.

give a lead correction to bring her forward. Be sure to praise after she adjusts position correctly.

As your dog progresses you should begin to *move at a constant speed* through the Figure Eight and let the dog adjust to your movements.

THE FINISH

In the Finish, you teach the dog, on command, to go to Heel from a sitting position in front of you.

There are two accepted methods of doing the Finish. The first is the "go around." In this method, you say the dog's name and give the Heel command. The dog then moves around your right side, crosses behind you and comes up to the Heel position at your left. The movement is very controlled and results in a straight Sit. I prefer this method.

Step 1: When first teaching the Finish, step back on your right foot to give the dog an additional cue to move around you.

The second method is a "Swing Finish," also called the "Poodle Finish." In this method, on command the dog moves to your left, approximately one pace past your left leg, and makes a tight counter-clockwise turn, comes up into the Heel position and sits.

Teaching the Go Around Finish

Step 1

To teach this Finish, have the dog on-lead and sitting at the Heel position. Give the verbal and hand command to Stay. Step out on the right foot and turn to face your dog. Place the lead in your right hand. Using your dog's name, give the command to Heel. With your right hand, smoothly pull your dog toward your right side. At the same time move your right foot back a half step. Continue to bring your dog around and behind you so that your right hand, which is holding the lead, is directly behind your back. Transfer the lead from the right hand to the left. Now continue to guide your dog around you with your left hand, bringing her up to your left side and into the Heel position.

Step 2: Transfer the lead from your right hand to the left as the dog comes around behind you.

Bring your right foot back up next to your left foot. (If necessary, particularly with a larger dog, you can take a step forward on your right foot, then bring your left foot forward and halt.)

As the dog moves into this position, switch the lead across in front of you to your right hand and say "Sit," guiding the dog into the Sit, if necessary, by gently snapping the lead up and slightly back. Remember, your dog is learning something new so don't overcorrect.

67

Step 3: Continue moving the dog around to the Heel position and into a straight Sit.

Once the dog has mastered this exercise on-lead and does it consistently, you are ready to practice off-lead.

Step 2

With the dog sitting at the Heel position off-lead, give the verbal command and hand signal to Stay. Step out on your right foot, turn and stand directly in front of your dog. Using her name, give the command Heel. To help a bit at the beginning, even though there is no lead, swing your right hand around your right side and behind you, in the same arc as when the dog was on-lead, and step back on your right foot a half step. The hand movement and the backward step encourage the dog to move around you. Continue the hand movement with your left hand as you did when using the lead, guiding the dog around the back of you and into the Heel position. Talk to your dog throughout these movements. It makes a difference when you are teaching a new exercise. All these extra cues are really helpful when the dog is learning, but be sure to eliminate them as soon as the dog no longer needs them. Remember to praise the dog.

The Swing Finish

Step 1

Sit your dog on-lead at the Heel position. Hold your lead in the left hand. Give the verbal command and hand signal Stay. Then step out on your right foot and turn and stand directly in front of your dog. Using your dog's name first, give the command Heel. With your left hand, smoothly pull your dog toward your left side and move your left foot back a half step. Keep the lead out almost an arm's length away from your body. Continue moving the dog past your extended left foot, and guide the dog with the lead in an arc—a tight counter-clockwise turn that brings the dog around beside you to the Heel position. Give a Sit command. Guide the dog into the Sit if necessary by pulling up and slightly backward on the lead. Be sure to praise enthusiastically.

Step 2

Once the dog has mastered this Finish on-lead, you can practice it off-lead. With the dog sitting at the Heel position, off-lead, give the dog the verbal command and hand signal Stay and step out directly in front. Turn and face her. Using her name, give the command Heel. To help at the beginning, I recommend you use your left hand, making the same hand movement as when the dog was on-lead to simulate the leash movement. At the same time bring your left foot back the half step, as before, to encourage your dog to continue moving. When she is far enough back, sweep the palm of your hand around so it faces front, still moving as if you were guiding her on-lead. Bring her up to the Heel position. Talk and encourage your dog to make the turn and come up to the Heel position and Sit. Don't forget to praise. The dog will have earned it.

If you have a problem with the Finish off-lead, go back on-lead until the dog more fully grasps the mechanics of the exercise.

As mentioned before, all the extra cues are helpful to the dog while learning. You should eliminate these extra cues, however, as soon as reasonable.

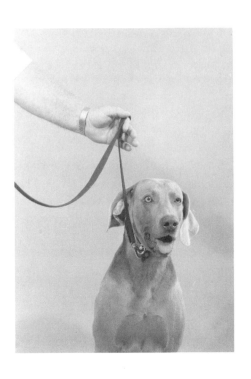

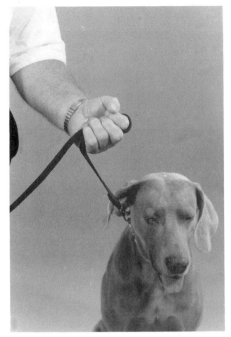

Wrist-twist Correction—grasp the lead firmly with the left hand and twist the wrist to a palm-upward position. How much "snap" you put into this correction depends on the size and temperament of your dog.

70

5

Correction and Praise

NO-CORRECTION CORRECTIONS

I believe it is better training to eliminate mistakes without overt correction, if possible. If, during training, you can correct errors that the dog is making in a positive way (such as the suggestion that you bring the lead around the back of you to correct when the dog sits forward), it makes for a happier working relationship. As with most undertakings, though, you have to think about what you are doing. I never like to see a handler setting a dog up to make an error so that the handler can pounce on the dog and make the correction.

Get to know your dog and understand what methods will bring out the best in him. That should be the goal of every dog handler. Only you can understand your dog well enough to know whether he needs gentle guidance or discipline and a firm hand. If your dog works well for you and turns in a good performance, you are handling well. If you are having learning and behavior problems with the dog, observe yourself in training sessions carefully. There is probably some handler error creeping into your training.

Whatever method of correction you find best for your dog, *don't nag*! You will be unintentionally training the dog to expect several commands. Let your dog know that the *first* command you give is the one that means business, *not* the second or third.

I must emphasize, however, that you can often get rid of a problem by appearing to ignore it. This may sound like a contradiction in terms. It isn't. Let me give you an example.

> **Problem:** When the handler comes to a Halt, the dog puts his paw down on top of the handler's foot.
>
> If your dog develops this habit, try this "correction." Keep your foot on the ground but raise your toe as high up in the air as you can. As the dog starts to put pressure on your foot, drop your toes suddenly and swing your foot aside out of his way. Don't look down at what you're doing. Don't say a word. After that happens a few times, he's going to be careful of your big, clumsy foot and give up. He'll forgive you for your awkwardness without any feelings of resentment!

MINIMIZE—DON'T MAXIMIZE

Remember, if you can stop a problem without making a big thing out of it, it is not going to stick in the dog's mind. Those things that have been emphasized over and over again are the ones that will stay. Just make this type of "no correction" correction without comment.

Almost all of us can remember something we did as a child for which we were soundly punished. We remember because our parents made it seem so important in our minds. They placed so much emphasis on it that it would be impossible to forget it.

People do this frequently with their dogs when they are training and then wonder why the error becomes so great a problem. If your dog is of a stubborn turn of mind, or if you've made the mistake of over-correcting repeatedly, he's going to resent it and keep repeating the error longer.

Use the covert method to correct problems before the error really becomes ingrained. This means paying close attention while working with the dog in the early stages of each exercise. If you have developed a problem, use the covert method before you use the more conventional methods of correction to any appreciable degree. If you have developed a chronic problem, this method will work, but it requires patience since it may take longer to get your message across.

If things are not going well in a particular exercise, try going back to one the dog does well. This may not seem like a correction technique, but it works. Build up the dog's confidence and give every appearance that you have forgotten the problem for the time being. Then return to it. It really isn't necessary to make a battle of wills out of every situation.

When you do use the no-punishment type of correction, *don't give the dog any sort of "Aha! Gotcha that time" comment or attitude.* Offer *no* comment and act as though the incident was an accident *no* matter how many times you may have to do it. The dog will get the message, but without any feeling of resentment.

RESENTMENT

Resentment is at the bottom of many problems. If a dog feels unfairly corrected, or corrected too severely, or even if he feels worked too long and hard, he will build up resentment to training. When you have a dog that knows what to do but won't do it, you will find frequently that resentment is the underlying cause.

To avoid this kind of stubbornness in training, *avoid resentment. A great deal of dog behavior that looks like stubbornness is in reality resentment behavior.* No dog will work well where strong feelings of resentment have been allowed to develop. Therefore, where it seems it will do some good, use your imagination. Try covert or no-punishment corrections.

I must emphasize that you must get to know your dog, to understand him and to keep the positive thought in your mind that you both are going to work harmoniously together. Negative thoughts get through to your dog. If you don't think much of him and expect a letdown, he'll get the message from you loud and clear. Make sure the messages are positive, messages that are going to help your dog give you the response you want, and give it in a cheerful, enthusiastic manner.

USING THE LEAD TO CORRECT

Corrections using the lead is a matter of timing. If you give a correction, it should be immediate. You must anticipate what your dog is going to do and whether this is going to be something wrong or something right. You must always be alert and ready to respond.

Correct timing for corrections includes such variables as how you pull the lead and how you snap the lead. Are you "telegraphing" corrections so that the dog knows to make an adjustment quickly? You may not get the correction you want. If you have too much lead hanging down, by the time you wind it up, your dog knows a correction is coming. If lagging, for instance, he may move up for the moment, but can then drop back again until the next "telegram" is on its way.

There are two methods of using the lead for corrections that are effective. Each one is used for a different purpose. The first is for corrections on the Sit exercise and the second is for general corrections where use of the lead is necessary.

The correction for the Sit exercise is described in that section but I will review it here. Hold the folded lead firmly in your right hand, at waist level. Be sure the dog has enough lead and is not forced to lean into you. But don't allow it to hang too loosely either. Then slide the left hand briskly down the lead. Don't grab or tug at it. Simply slide the left hand quickly down the lead until it stops behind, *but is not hitting*, the dog's neck. Your hand stops behind the neck giving the lead a firm snap. With this correction for the Sit exercise you are able to keep the dog properly situated and balanced.

The other type of correction with the lead I call a "wrist-twist." All you do is turn the wrist. Again, hold the folded lead in the right hand at waist level. The left hand is hanging down at your side, holding the lead lightly. When the correction is called for, grasp the lead firmly with the left hand and twist the wrist to a palm-upward position.

As you turn the wrist, press your elbow downward and a bit forward into your side to get a bit of a snap into it. That's all there is to it. Be sure, however, that your dog's collar is fitted properly so he doesn't get hit in the eye with the snap swivel when you give a correction.

It is important with this type of correction to be aware of your own strength. This correction is adequate for the largest dog so you must tone it down to meet the size and needs if your own dog is smaller.

You must judge what is the best correction for your dog. Your criterion must be what brings out the best in the dog and develops a spirit of cooperation. Never think that you can develop a happy, working, cooperative dog by browbeating. It just isn't so. There *may* be times, however, when your dog needs a firm hand. It would simply be unrealistic to pretend that it can never happen. When it does, it is well to be properly prepared.

"LIVE" RING VS. "DEAD" RING

The question of whether to attach the lead to the "live" ring or the "dead" ring seems to arise naturally here. A basic part of my philosophy of dog training is the belief that when you are teaching the dog something new, you never give a punishment type of correction. You work on the dead ring. If you are reviewing something the dog knows but needs a little sharpening up on, use the live ring. If your dog is really giving you the business and knows what you want but just isn't going to do it, one firm correction on the live ring of the collar might be more effective than a lot of lesser corrections.

Understand your dog's needs. Some never need the live ring correction. Some need it occasionally. Some need constant discipline until they shape up into responsible canine citizens. A helpful suggestion might be to use the dead ring as much as possible, resorting to the live ring only after careful consideration and a calm evaluation of the problem. If discipline is required, use it, but don't switch to the live ring just because things are not working well and you're feeling hot under the collar.

If you're not familiar with the terms "live" and "dead" rings, let me review the terms. When you put the collar on the dog, you hold it like the letter *P* turned on its side. The ring on the end that you hold in your left hand is the "live" ring. The "dead" ring is the ring that slides along the collar. I use and recommend the "dead" ring for most training situations. This is more than adequate for almost all cases. The live ring should only be used when strong correction is called for. Some problems are temporary. In that case, use the live ring for a short time if necessary.

Some dogs turn into difficult "teenagers" around a year and a half of age, and can test your patience. They start trying to get the upper hand. The live ring may be required here for a period of time. And then there is the stubborn dog who locks his knees and dares you to move him. Also, there are dogs who are not easily trained and never will be. The live ring must be used most of the time for a dog with this kind of an attitude. But let me tell you, when you want to deliver a correction, you should never underestimate the power of the spoken word. A few well-chosen words in an authoritative tone that demands respect can work wonders. If you are having serious problems with your dog, combine the voice with the live ring corrections to remind your dog who is the boss.

PRAISING YOUR DOG

Let us consider how to praise your dog when training. A handler cannot effusively praise a dog constantly and expect that praise to have much meaning after a while. It's simply too much of a good thing. Words of praise should be saved for the times when they are appropriate. As you work, do not drown your dog in endless displays of affection and constant empty praise.

Praise is definitely required when the dog has done well during training sessions. Since your dog really desires to please you, it is as important to communicate praise when he's done something *right* as quickly as you let him know when he's done something wrong. A few well-placed words of praise make the dog feel capable of all those wonderful things you expect.

When praising, even though you may be one of those handlers who enjoy the solid feel of your dog, please don't pound with a heavy hand. Don't pound on the dog's back or chest, rough him up or pull him affectionately into your legs. When the dog is sitting beside you, a brisk rub on the *right* shoulder and a few kind words are enough. It keeps the dog sitting straight and makes him feel good all at the same time.

This might be a good place to caution you about praising your dog when your training session is over. Don't immediately rush into praises or play. Keep the dog under control, because if you decide to go to a show and the judge says "Exercise finished," you don't want the dog to dash out of the ring in great good spirits, as he will be penalized. Move away from the training area or show ring in a controlled manner. Once away from your "business address," give the dog some time to relax and play.

6

The Stay Exercises

THE LONG SIT AND RETURN

This exercise is a progressive one. You begin with a five-to-thirty-second Long Sit with the dog on-lead. Your final goal is to have the dog remain sitting off-lead as you walk away, stand at a distance of thirty feet for a full minute and then return.

Step 1

Begin with the dog on-lead in the Heel position, sitting at your side. Without using the dog's name, give the verbal Stay command. You do not use the dog's name when you are doing stationary exercises. This will be a cue to your dog that she is not required to move. Add the Stay hand signal.

Pause for a moment after giving the command and then walk away from the dog. Start off on your right foot. Right foot means the dog stays in place. (She only moves off with you when you start off on the left foot.) Gradually build up the distance until you go out to the end of the lead.

When you move away from the dog, make it a positive-looking movement. Don't edge away. That looks like a game and can cause odd reactions. Walk at a normal pace. Appear confident that the dog will remain in place.

Introducing the Long Down on lead. Keep the lead loose. Do not look directly at the dog.

Still holding the lead, turn and face your dog. Do not make direct eye contact with the dog. This can cause her to break the command and come to you (because that's where she likes to be).

If the dog shows any signs of moving, be alert! Be prepared to give a verbal command to Stay or an ''Ah-ah'' to remind the dog to remain sitting. To reinforce your command, raise your right hand and give the Stay hand signal.

If this fails to keep your dog on the Stay and she does move, or lie down, pull sharply upward on the lead, giving it a good snap. Again, give the commands Sit and Stay. Your voice should be firm and authoritative. There should be no doubt in the dog's mind that you are displeased. If you have a problem with the dog chronically breaking the Sit/Stay, do not go all the way out to the end of the lead. Work closer so that you can get the correction in quickly. Wait fifteen to thirty seconds.

Then return to your dog. Walk back at a normal pace. Go around the left side and behind her, and come up to the Heel position. Handle the lead carefully, keeping it out of your dog's face. Do not let her move yet. Stand there quietly and slowly count off five or ten seconds. Then give the dog's name and the command Heel. Take two steps forward and halt. At this point the dog should sit again. The purpose of the two steps is to accustom the dog to the idea that *you choose when to end the exercise*.

This concept of having the dog *heel two steps at the end of an exercise is a building block* that will prove to be invaluable in Open work. By keeping the dog on command at the end of an exercise at this stage of training, you reduce the tendency to break commands prematurely in Open work.

After returning to your dog, pause a few seconds. Do not allow the dog to get up until you give the command to Heel.

Vary the amount of time you take before giving the Heel command so that the dog doesn't begin anticipating. When you have completed the exercise, be sure to praise your dog.

Extend the time the dog holds the Sit position gradually. Once the dog is steady on the Sit/Stay on-lead and holds the position for a full minute, you can begin to make the transition to a Long Sit off-lead.

Step 2—The Transition

With the dog on-lead at the Heel position, sitting at your side, turn the dog's collar around so that the snap swivel is lying on the back of the dog's neck, placing a slight pressure on the collar. *Lay the lead down in back of the dog.*

Tell your dog to Stay, giving the hand signal as well, and step off on the right foot. Turn and *stand directly in front of her*. By standing this close, the dog does not immediately realize that you are not holding the lead. Keep your hands relaxed at your sides. Don't stare directly at her. If the dog begins to move, give the verbal command and hand signal Stay. Remain standing there for fifteen to twenty seconds. Then return around your dog to the Heel position. Do not let the dog move when you return. Count off a few seconds, give the dog's name and the command Heel. Take two steps forward and halt. Be sure to give the dog a lot of praise for her efforts.

If the dog either gets up or lies down, give a correction immediately. Take her by the back of the collar and firmly say "Sit/Stay." If your dog has moved off the spot where she was sitting, be sure to put her back on the Sit/Stay in *exactly* the same spot as before.

This exercise should be repeated in this transition method until the dog holds the position without moving, for at least thirty seconds. When she is able to do that, it's time to progress to the next level.

Step 3

Have the dog on-lead in the Heel position sitting at your side. Then, using as light a hand as possible, remove the lead from the collar. Be as unobtrusive as you can. Then dangle the snap swivel at the dog's side, *giving the impression that it is still connected to the collar.*

Give the dog the Stay command along with the Stay hand signal. Pause, facing forward, for a second or two. Then starting with your right foot, walk about six feet from the dog, *laying the lead along the floor as you go.* Turn and face the dog. The lead is now lying on the floor in a line between you and the dog.

If your dog starts to move, be right there with a verbal correction: "Ah-ah, don't do that!" Give the command Stay. As soon as you see so much as a muscle twitch, *respond!* That's good timing. While training, it is important that your total attention be on the dog to anticipate problems and be ready to make a correction. *Be alert! Don't wait for the dog to make a mistake. When you see your dog even start to think about it, give that correction.*

If the dog has already started moving, return quickly. Put her back in position and give the command Stay. This time, don't move away. If she needs additional correction, you'll be right there. Then move back in gradual stages.

As the dog becomes more stable on the Sit without the lead, increase the distance to approximately ten to fifteen feet. Also, try to increase the sitting time to a full minute. It is important that you remain alert to any movements of the dog so that you can give a correction immediately. If she remains stable over several training sessions extend the distance to the full thirty feet.

When the dog is stable at that distance, you can then practice the exercise in the same manner that you would do it if you were in the show ring.

Step 4

With the dog sitting at your side, give both the verbal command and hand signal Stay. Pause for a moment or two, then leave your dog, stepping off on your right foot. Walk briskly away from your dog for a distance of thirty feet.

Turn and face your dog. You must remain stationary for the period of time that you are away from your dog, so stand comfortably. Do not stare directly at the dog.

When the one-minute period has elapsed, walk at a moderate pace toward your dog. Don't look at her, as it may cause her to get up. Walk around the dog to the Heel position. Count off five or ten seconds. Then tell your dog to Heel. Take two steps forward and halt. Praise your dog for her efforts.

It is good to vary the amount of time that you practice this exercise. Let the dog sit from a half minute to a minute and a half. Dogs have a good sense of timing. You don't want your dog to get so used to the one minute Sit that she starts anticipating.

THE LONG DOWN AND RETURN

In this exercise your goal is to have the dog lie down and stay in place for three minutes with the handler standing at a distance of approximately thirty feet. In Novice AKC Obedience Trials, there will usually be a row of dogs lined up for this exercise. However, with the new AKC rules, there is the possibility that you and your dog may have to go into the ring alone to do this exercise. Therefore, although you will train this exercise in a group, you must also practice with the dog working alone.

The dog must lie with her body in a straight line, and should not curve to the left or right, nor lie on her side. *Your dog is not there to take a nap* she should be lying at attention.

The exercise is taught in stages. The distance gradually builds to thirty feet. Your time increases from thirty seconds to three minutes.

Since the dog is familiar with the Sit/Stay command, teaching the Down/Stay should follow naturally.

Step 1

With the dog sitting on-lead at the Heel position, give the Down command and the hand signal for the Down as well. Then give the Stay command and the Stay hand signal.

Pause for a moment or two. Then starting off on your right foot, walk to the end of the lead. Turn and face your dog. Do not make direct eye contact with the dog. Rather look over the top of her head. Direct eye contact might invite some dogs to edge toward you. To other dogs, it might seem intimidating. Either way, it is apt to cause them to break the Down position.

Keep track of the time. During your training sessions you want to gradually increase the time the dog is down, from thirty seconds until you reach a full three minutes. At this point, however, you are working in the thirty-second to one-minute range.

If the dog at any time shows signs of rolling over, creeping toward you or moving in any direction, be prepared to give the verbal command Stay or an "ah-ah" to remind her to remain down. At the same time raise your right hand and give the hand signal Stay—hand raised, palm turned outward toward the dog.

When you are ready to return to your dog, walk along her left side, completely around behind and up to the Heel position. Don't let her move immediately. Count off five or ten seconds. Then give the dog's name and the command to Heel. Starting on the left foot, take two steps forward and halt.

Once you have the dog steady on the Down on-lead for about a full minute or two, begin to train without the lead.

Step 2

With the dog on-lead sitting at the Heel position, give the Down command and hand signal. Then using a light hand, remove the snap swivel from the collar. Do not let it be obvious to the dog that you have removed the lead. *Dangle the snap swivel at the dog's side, giving the impression that it is still connected to the collar.*

After you give the dog the Down verbal command and hand signal, tell her Stay, again using both the verbal command and the hand signal. Walk approximately six feet away from the dog, stepping off on the right foot.

As you step off, lay the lead out in front of you on the floor or ground so that when you turn to face the dog the lead is fully stretched out between you. If the dog breaks the Down, immediately return, picking up the lead as you go. Go around behind the dog and come up in the Heel position. Take hold of the collar and put her back in the Down position. Firmly give the Down and Stay commands along with the hand signal. Speak in an authoritative voice, letting your dog know that you are displeased. Once she is down again, repeat the exercise. If you feel it is necessary, you can put her back on-lead again and work back up to this point.

82

Step 3

In this step, take the lead off the training collar and pass the lead, loop first, through the collar toward the hindquarters of the dog. Then hold the snap swivel end and the loop end in your left hand. Fold the lead into your hand so that only enough slack is left to make the lead short enough to control the dog.

With the dog sitting at the Heel position, give the Down command and hand signal. Then as you give both the verbal and hand signal Stay, you gently pull the lead out of the collar. You don't want the dog to be aware of what you have done. Taking the lead with you, move off on your right foot about six feet forward. Drape the lead around your neck and turn and face your dog. Keep your hands naturally at your side. Look toward the dog, but do not make eye contact.

The first time or two, keep the dog on the command no more than fifteen to thirty seconds. Work up to a minute. It is important to end this exercise on a successful note. So don't try to extend the time beyond the dog's present capabilities.

If she does break the Down, return briskly. Walk around in back of your dog to the Heel position. Take the collar in your left hand and put her back down. Give the Down and Stay commands. Say each command with authority. Your voice and attitude should make it obvious that you're *displeased*, but *not angry*.

This is a pivotal level in teaching this exercise. If, at this point, the dog holds the Down in a steady manner with only minor errors, it is time to move forward. If you are having trouble with your dog at this level, I recommend that you return to the previous step and work from there.

Step 4

This exercise begins with the dog sitting at the Heel position off-lead. The folded lead is placed a short distance behind the dog, as you would in the show ring. Make sure your dog is sitting properly. If she isn't, give a Heel command, turn in a circle with the dog and sit her again.

When the dog is sitting properly, give both the verbal Down command and the Down hand signal. Once the dog is down, give the hand signal Stay.

Leave your dog, and start off on your right foot. Walk away briskly from your dog to a distance of approximately fifteen feet. Turn and face her. You can, if you wish, fold your arms or place them behind your back if you find one of these positions comfortable. If not, your arms should remain naturally at your sides because this is the Recall position. I suggest folding your arms or placing them behind your back before turning to face the dog. Remember not to stare at the dog.

Be prepared to give a verbal correction if your dog begins to move. If she gets up, quickly approach the dog from the front, take the collar in your left hand and give it an upward snap as you turn the dog around and reposition her in the Heel position. Give the command Sit, then give the Down and Stay commands. *Use a very firm voice.* Let her know that you are displeased. Work at this level until your dog becomes stable. Then gradually move out from her to a full thirty feet away.

If your dog rolls over, breaks to come to you or sits up as you increase the distance, there are several things you can do to correct this problem.

PROBLEM SOLVING

A Board Can Help

Try using a Broad Jump board placed on its side in front of the dog. Any similar type board will work as well as long as it is held upright securely. This is often enough to keep the dog in place.

A Hidden Correction

This requires someone to help you. Take a twenty-foot piece of curtain cord or any other lightweight rope—no more than a-quarter-of an inch in diameter. Tie a lightweight snap swivel to one end. Remove the dog's six-foot lead and replace it with the rope. Attach it to the live ring.

Sit the dog next to you in the Heel position (or the Down position, whichever the dog is having the most trouble holding). Give the rope to a helper and have them quietly go to the rear of the dog, about halfway the length of the rope. The handler gives the dog a Stay command and steps out on the right foot, to about 15 feet in front, and facing the dog. If the dog starts to get fidgety or even thinks about changing its position, the helper "snaps" the lead straight back while giving a voice correction and immediately lets the rope go slack. *It is important that the correction be straight back and not upward.* The handler returns to the dog, scolding but not intimidating. The dog knows that the handler didn't make "it" happen. It creates the idea in the dog's mind that if she or he breaks a command, there will be a "surprise" correction coming, even if the handler doesn't seem to be holding the lead.

This is a very effective method of correction. However, like other training aids, it should be used when needed and eliminated from use as quickly as possible.

STAND FOR EXAMINATION—ON-LEAD

There are two parts to this exercise. In the first part, the dog must Stand and Stay on command. In the second part, your dog learns to remain quietly in this position while her head, body and hindquarters are touched. The dog should not display any shyness or resentment.

Stand and Stay

When first teaching this exercise, use a lead. However, when you do the exercise in the Obedience ring, realize that the exercise must be done off-lead.

Walk the dog into position to begin this exercise. Heel the dog along on a shortened lead for a few steps, then stop, giving a Stand command. Hold the lead in your right hand. Turning toward the dog, use your left hand, palm downward, fingers together, to lightly touch the front of the dog's right rear leg. Your hand barely touches the dog's underside.

Note that the Stand command and the hand movement are done together. Switch the lead back to your left hand. Pause a few seconds, and with your right hand, give a Stay command and hand signal. As you move away from the dog, keep the lead loose. This is important. If you don't keep a loose lead, you are apt to pull your dog out of the Stand position. Step off on your right foot and walk forward approximately six feet. Then turn and face your dog.

One of the nice features of walking the dog into a Stand is that there is little reason to touch her. Once the exercise is learned, and the dog becomes aware that she may have to remain in the Stand position for some time, her feet will go into a comfortable position without any prodding by you. Furthermore, it is impressive to have your dog literally *glide* into a Stand. It is a further statement to the judge that you are in control of your dog.

Conformation and Obedience Application

Some handlers who are planning to show their dog in Conformation as well as in Obedience find this method unsatisfactory. Their concern is that the breed protocol requires the dog to be posed in a specified manner, and that teaching the dog the exercise in this way may cause the handler some difficulty in posing the dog properly.

In that case, stand the dog by holding the collar with your right hand and use the edge of your left hand against the upper part of the dog's right rear leg. Give the Stand command and Stay verbal and hand commands and continue on with the exercise. The handler has the option of standing or posing the dog, so select the method with which you are most comfortable.

TRAINING AIDS FOR THE STAND FOR EXAMINATION

The Board

If you have a problem keeping the dog in place on the Stand, place a Broad Jump or board on its side in front of the dog. If necessary, secure it with cinder blocks or anything that will keep it from toppling. For a really small breed, place the Utility bar under the dog so she doesn't move or try to lie down. Stand the very large dog over the number one board of the Broad Jump, turned on its side. If your dog continually lies down on the Stand, try putting a grooming brush under her to break the habit.

The Sling

Some dogs just don't respond well to the conventional method of teaching the Stand. It would seem that the more physical contact you make with the dog, the more "wiggly" they become no matter what you do. In this instance, use your lead as a "sling" to get the dog to stand.

With the dog on-lead and the collar on the dead ring, position your dog in front of you with her head toward your right shoulder.

When teaching the Stand for Examination standing the dog over a board will inhibit moving or lying down.

Using your right hand, hold the lead approximately twelve inches out from the dog's collar. Take the loop end of the lead and drape it over the left side of the dog. Then draw the lead under the dog toward you to form a sling. Take hold of both ends of the lead in your left hand and raise the ends upward to exert a slight pressure on the underside of the dog. Make sure that the sling is far enough back so that the dog can stand comfortably.

In a quiet voice tell the dog Stand/Stay. Once she begins to respond to the exercise, praise. Gradually eliminate the use of the sling and return to the conventional method of teaching the Stand exercise.

THE EXAMINATION

You are now standing six feet out in front of your dog, who is on a Stand/Stay command. Examine your own dog if you don't have a helper. Hold the lead in your left hand and walk back to the dog at a normal pace.

As you approach, move your left arm away from your body slightly so that you are able to keep the lead out of the dog's face. If

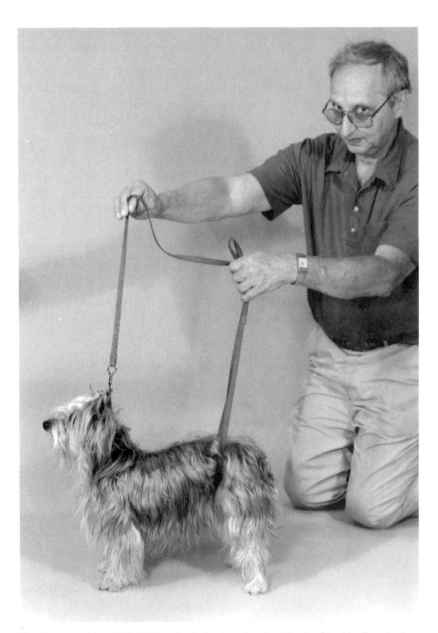

The sling—a training aid that helps steady the dog when teaching the Stand for Examination.

the lead gets in her face, she may break the Stand. Stop an arm's length away from the dog. Palm down, slowly present your right hand to the dog. Holding your hand in front of the dog's nose, let her sniff it. She should not move. If she stands quietly, give praise. If she moves, say "S-t-a-y" in a normal tone of voice.

Then use your right hand to lightly touch the dog's head for a moment. Next you begin to move around the right side of the dog, keeping the lead over to the left, out of her face. With the palm of your hand, gently touch her back and hindquarters. If there is any sign of the dog moving, in a gentle voice give the Stay command. Continue moving around the dog and come up to the Heel position. The dog should remain standing calmly in place, with you now alongside.

Starting on the right foot, continue out the full length of the lead, turn and face your dog. To steady her, you can give an extra Stand/Stay command. Remain standing there for several seconds. Then go back around the dog to the Heel position. Pause a few seconds. Then use the dog's name and give the Heel command. Starting on the left foot, take two steps forward and halt. Praise her for her efforts—even if they were less than perfect.

Once you can examine your own dog without difficulty, you can have someone the dog is familiar with perform the examination. When another person examines your dog, you remain standing at the end of the lead. Have your "examiner" walk up to the dog normally. Let the dog sniff his or her right hand. The examination continues in exactly the same way as when you did it yourself. The dog is touched lightly on the head, midsection and hindquarters. The examiner should not hover over the dog. The examination should not be rushed. When done, the examiner should walk around the dog and back out in front of her about six feet. The dog should stand quietly throughout.

At this point you return to the dog, still keeping the lead out of her face, and come to the Heel position. Vary the length of time you wait between five and ten seconds before returning to the dog. This helps to prevent the dog from anticipating.

Keep the dog in the Stand position for several seconds as well. Then give the command Heel and, starting on your left foot, take two steps forward and halt. Praise your dog for her efforts. It is well deserved.

IF THE DOG DISPLAYS SHYNESS

If the dog displays timidity or shyness, I have found this to be a socialization problem in most cases. The dog that displays nervous behavior, more often than not, does not get an opportunity to encounter a variety of people, or experience new places.

If you are taking your dog to school, get there early. Get right in the middle of things. Stand with the dog where it is going to get crowded—at the door, near a water fountain, anywhere where a number of people will be milling around.

Don't appear to pay attention to your dog. Don't tighten up on the lead. Most important of all, when you begin, *don't tell everyone you're working on socialization.* If you do, well-meaning dog lovers will want to pet and fuss over the dog. An inexperienced dog will back away from that and it won't solve the problem.

Initially, just stand where it is busy. When the dog gets used to that and relaxes, arrange to have someone walk toward the dog as though for examination. But instead of stopping, have them keep walking past the dog.

Next, someone can walk up to the dog, look over the top of her and bend down slightly—just walking past, talking to themselves. Don't tighten up on the lead. Keep the dog relaxed.

Then vary things. Have the person touch the dog while walking past. Next time, have someone go by without touching the dog. In either case, the person shouldn't look directly at the dog.

Don't let anyone tower over the dog. That is intimidating. If they are going to touch the dog, they should just bend slightly to do so. Have them give the dog a word or two of praise.

The whole idea is to socialize the dog without having people force themselves on the dog. Everything should seem accidental and very casual.

Then, when the dog is ready, let one of the instructors walk up to the dog in the same way and begin touching her. After a few tries, give the dog a Stay command and have the instructor give a little more of an examination. To help the dog realize that there is nothing to be frightened of, work up to the full examination gradually.

It also helps to take the dog on outings whenever possible. If she encounters a strange situation or noises that makes her shy away, give lots of reassurance. After a few outings, you should begin to see a significant improvement in the dog's attitude, and in addition, performance on this exercise should improve.

7

Heeling Off-Lead

COMING OFF-LEAD

Frequently, handlers decide that their dogs are ready to work off-lead too soon. Having your dog heel off-lead gives a wonderful feeling of progress, but unless he is really ready for it, your success isn't going to last very long.

Keep the lead on until the dog is heeling well consistently, without correction. The key word in that sentence is *consistently*. Take time to be absolutely certain that your dog is ready for off-lead Heeling. Shortcuts are costly in time and effort.

The transition from on-lead heeling to off-lead Heeling involves a series of steps. There is no precise timetable. The only measure is how well the dog responds to the transition exercises. Some dogs move through all of them relatively quickly; others at some point take more time. Don't be in a big hurry. Enjoy the process of training. If you have taught your dog well to Heel on-lead, you have every reason to expect him to Heel well off-lead.

As a safety measure, when you are training, it is essential that this transition be made in a controlled area such as a fenced-in yard, a basement area or a garage. In addition, when you begin, the use of plumber's helpers will make your job more successful. A full description of the plumber's helpers follows this section.

When you begin Heeling off-lead, mental attitude plays an important role. You must appear confident that the dog will do what you expect. It is imperative that you pay attention to what is happening at every moment. Also, you must keep your dog's undivided attention. Don't Heel too slowly. Find the speed at which your dog comes to life. That will help keep him at your side.

Walk straight and keep your feet out of your dog's way. Staying out of the way of sloppy footwork by the handler is one of the biggest causes of lagging in off-lead Heeling.

Keep in mind also that your left leg is the guide leg. Don't slap at it excessively in an effort to keep the dog in position beside you. The more you do it, the more he'll wait for it. Use this cue no more than necessary.

Your hands should remain relaxed at your sides, not in the dog's face. Don't give the dog the impression that you are reaching to give a correction.

If you move your shoulders to the right or the left, or shift your hips, you will see your dog cueing off these movements. The dog sees and reacts to body language as well as voice. If you drop your hip and shoulder back, it looks as though a turn is coming and the dog hangs back. Keep your shoulders and hips aligned in order to avoid unintentionally training the dog to lag.

It is surprising how often the handler is totally unaware of giving cues. Don't confuse the dog. Be aware of your posture, movements and voice. Be sure you are giving the dog the correct message at all times.

If your dog is lagging, and you believe it is not handler error, try attaching a rather heavy snap swivel on the dog's collar. The weight alone acts as a reminder to stay in position.

The clothes you wear in training are important. Don't wear clothes that get in the way. Don't have your dog walking under large full skirts or alongside extra-wide pants. Wear well-fitted shoes. The dog will begin Heeling wide to avoid distractions. When you train, do everything possible not to put your dog at a disadvantage.

TRANSITIONAL STEPS TO OFF-LEAD HEELING

Step 1

While Heeling in a straight line with the dog on-lead, put the lead over your left shoulder instead of holding it in the usual way. Leave enough slack in the lead so that there is no tension on the dog's collar.

Allow your arms to swing naturally at your sides. Do a short heeling routine, with Left and Right turns and About Turns. Be sure to keep sufficient slack in the lead so you don't inadvertently pull the dog.

If the dog strays from the Heel position by going wide, lagging or forging, use your left hand to make an appropriate correction with the lead. Then, using the dog's name, give the command Heel. You want your dog to know that the lead is still there. Work this way until he is Heeling well when the lead is over your shoulder. Then you are ready to move along to the next step.

Step 2

In this step, you want unobtrusively to slide the lead off the dog while Heeling. To do this, slide the loop end of the lead through the dog's collar from front to back. Hold the *snap swivel* in your left hand and hang the loop end on the little finger of your left hand. Fold up the excess lead. Leave enough lead hanging down so that it is not taut, but no more than that. Using the dog's name, give the Heel command. As you walk along, drop the loop off your little finger and pull it up and out of the collar without letting the dog know what you are doing. Be sure to *drop the loop end, not the snap swivel* so you don't hit the dog with it. Try to remove the lead without letting your dog know what you are doing. Once you have taken the lead off, dangle the snap swivel next to him, giving the impression he is still on-lead.

As you make a series of Left and Right turns and About Turns, you will get a good idea if you have the dog under control. Keep up enthusiastic comments to hold his attention. If the dog strays from the Heel position, give a firm verbal correction. Praise when he moves back into position.

Step 3

Your final step is to slide the loop end of the lead through the collar. Hold the snap swivel in your left hand and hang the loop end over your little finger. Fold the excess lead in your hand. As you begin heeling forward for a few paces, again drop the loop end of the lead off your finger and pull the lead out of the collar as unobtrusively as possible. Either stuff the lead in your pocket or hang it around your neck. Don't ball the lead up in your fist. Try to keep the dog from noticing what you have done with the lead.

As you drop the lead off your finger and pull up it up and out of the collar, use the dog's name and give a firm-sounding Heel command.

To make the transition to off-lead Heeling, slide the loop end of the lead through the collar from front to back. Hold the snap swivel in the left hand and hang the loop over the little finger. As you Heel, drop the loop off your finger and unobtrusively pull it out of the dog's collar.

94

You want the dog to focus on the command and miss the fact that the lead has come off and disappeared and that he is Heeling off-lead. Don't overdo this exercise. At first, keep the sessions short so that you don't lose your dog's attention. End the sessions on a high note. Always give praise for the dog's efforts when you are done and then put him back on-lead. In the beginning you only want your dog off-lead for short periods of time in controlled circumstances.

If at any time your dog goes out of control on the off-lead Heeling exercise, put him back on-lead and start out again.

Some handlers in training like to use bells or a toy when Heeling off-lead to keep the dog attentive and in position. I don't really think you need to use them. Frequently, the handler is the cause of the problems that arise. It's better to correct handler error than compensate with toys or bells.

If you lack the confidence in your dog's Heeling and keep looking down or back to check on the dog's position, the dog gets the impression something is going to happen. If your shoulder or hips drop back, it's only natural for the dog to see this as a cue and think you are going to turn. Therefore, he stays back and starts lagging. It is important to *remember how significant body cues are to your dog.*

If you begin experiencing significant problems while Heeling off-lead, go back on-lead. There are handlers who don't want to do this because they feel it is going backward in training and is a waste of time. This is not so. This is the way you will find those errors that are creating the problem. The errors may be made by the dog or by the handler. In either case go back on-lead and pay attention as you work through the steps outlined above.

PLUMBER'S HELPERS (THE CHUTE)

The plumber's helpers, or chute, is a very useful aid that helps to control the dog in several ways. It keeps him in a confined area when you start heeling off-lead and discourages the dog from running off. I recommend that you begin off-lead Heeling using this helpful training aid.

The plumber's helper is a simple device, made up of two sets of six plumber's plungers each. They are strung together on thin cord and spaced about four feet apart. The end plungers should be weighted. Holes are drilled in the handles and three or four lines of cord are run through them. They are each approximately twenty feet long. When

When you begin Heeling off lead, use the Plumber's Helpers to keep the dog at your side.

you use a double row of them, placed four feet apart, they create a chute. If you use a single row of plumber's helpers, it can be placed four feet from a wall or fence.

You can also use plain wooden dowels in the same way. Simply insert them into the ground. Dowels made of metal pipe set in weighted bases can also be used to achieve the same results.

Be sure to walk the dog through the chute on-lead to familiarize him with it. Once comfortable with the idea of the chute, you can begin training the dog here off-lead. Initially, you might want to have people stationed at either end to be sure the dog doesn't walk in one end and out the other. If you don't have any helpers, barriers placed at either end will do.

Heel the dog into the chute before removing the lead. Then practice off-lead Heeling in the chute as suggested, gradually removing

NOVICE HEELING PATTERN

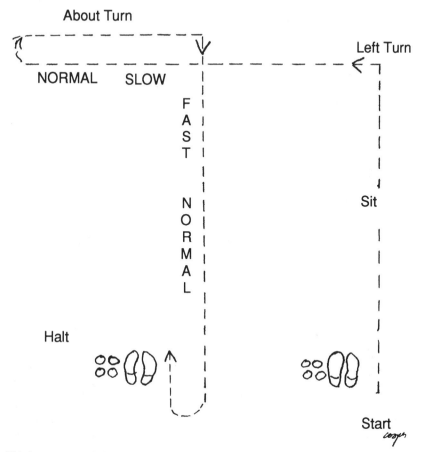

This is a suggested Heeling pattern that incorporates all of the elements of Heeling, and prepares you for the type of pattern you may encounter in AKC competition.

the lead by stages. Work in the chute until the dog remains beside you, and *you* gain confidence.

In addition to the off-lead Heeling exercise, you can work at other exercises such as Sit/Stays, Down/Stays and Recalls in the chute as well.

On the Recall, as the dog comes in to you, hold an imaginary "bubble" in front of you and raise it to waist height. As the dog looks upward, you will get a straight Sit.

8

The Recall

IN THE RECALL, you ask your dog to *break* a Sit/Stay command, and while you are standing at a distance, have her come to you. Initially, you use a technique that does not require the dog break the Sit/Stay command. After that, your dog will learn that, although on a Sit/Stay, in this instance for the Recall exercise, she is to come to you on command.

This exercise will be taught in several steps since it is a somewhat complicated exercise. Read through the instructions a few times to get the overall picture of what you will be doing and your final goal.

It is important that when the dog comes in to you, she should be enthusiastic and with a gait that is upbeat and brisk. The dog that walks slowly or erratically is an embarrassment. How you train will make all the difference in the world. *Never punish the dog when she comes in to you*. This will make any dog reluctant to get near you. Give plenty of praise and encouragement as you work on these component parts. Make sure your dog wants to come to you as quickly and as cheerfully as possible.

TEACHING THE EXERCISE

Step 1—The Sit in Front

To start teaching this exercise, begin by walking with the dog on-lead. *Give no Heel commands.* As you are walking along, quickly step back and call the dog's name. As she turns and faces you, go back a few more steps and give the Come command. As you give the command, give the lead a short snap to get your dog moving toward you.

As the dog comes in close to you, give the Sit command. If she does not come in straight, keep taking a few more steps backward so that you get a straight Sit. Be sure to praise. It will motivate the dog to come to you. As you can see, using this method when you begin training doesn't break the Sit/Stay command.

Step 2—Recall On-Lead

Now that the dog has gotten the idea that you want her to come and sit in front of you, it's time to teach *breaking* the Sit/Stay command.

Put the dog on a Sit/Stay and move out to the end of the lead. Turn and face the dog. Keep the lead loose so there is no tension on the dog's collar. Hold the lead in your right hand. Before you call the dog by name and give the Come command, wait five to ten seconds to avoid anticipation by the dog. You don't want her to get up and come to you prematurely.

When you say the name and the command Come, give the lead a snap if necessary to encourage the dog to come. Talk enthusiastically and in an upbeat voice to provide added motivation.

Remember, you have just given your dog the command Stay—and now you are asking her to *break that command and respond to a second command.* This can be confusing. If the dog doesn't move on the first command, give another Come command and a second tug on the lead. Give *plenty* of verbal encouragement. At the beginning, do what it takes to make your dog want to come to you. If necessary, try taking a few steps backward. The motion will encourage her to move toward you.

It is important, right from the start, that the dog comes *straight to you.* The straighter the line of approach, the more likely you will get a good Sit. If the dog is not coming in straight, or starts to run past you, take a few additional steps backward.

The Bubble

The bubble will help the dog to sit squarely in front of you. As she comes in to you, cup your hands in front of you as though you are holding a big bubble. Start approximately at knee height and raise your hands to chest height. Don't move too quickly. You want the dog to follow your hand movement. As she watches your hands moving upward, your dog will look up and sit automatically.

The dog should not bump into your legs or paw you as she sits, nor sit too far from you. The dog must sit close enough to you so that you could remove an object from her mouth without moving forward or stretching.

If your dog comes to you and stands rather than sits in front of you, it is imperative that you do *not* punish her. You don't want to lose your dog's confidence and make her shy of coming near you for fear of reprimand. If she doesn't sit, or if the Sits are not perfect, it is much smarter to praise for coming to you, because she did that part right. Stop and play for a minute or so, and then begin the exercise again. This time you can work on a correct Sit. *Use encouragement to teach, rather than constant corrections.*

When teaching this exercise, focus on getting the dog to come to you and to sit squarely in front of you. Do not incorporate the Finish into the exercise as yet.

For now, when the dog sits in front of you, *you* should be the one to go to the Heel position. Tell your dog Stay and give the hand signal as well. Then walk around behind the dog and come up into the Heel position. You then pause a moment or two, say the dog's name and give the command Heel. Step off on your left foot, take two steps and halt.

Step 3

At this point, you are ready to work off-lead. With the dog sitting at the Heel position, remove the lead. Slide the loop end of the lead through the dog's collar from front to back. Hold the snap swivel in your left hand along with the excess lead folded neatly. Leave just enough lead hanging down so that it is not taut.

Give the verbal Stay command and hand signal. Walk out to the end of the lead, letting the folds of the lead out, but still holding the snap swivel end. When you get to the end of the lead, turn and face the dog. The loop end of the lead is still tucked in the dog's collar.

Count off a few seconds—you don't want the dog to anticipate the command. Using the dog's name, tell her Come. Tug the lead out of the collar as you take several steps backward. The dog is now off-lead and moving toward you.

Smile. Clap your hands. Give verbal encouragement. These are the things that will get your dog bounding toward you with enthusiasm. You can again use the imaginary bubble movement to get her to sit directly in front of you. Use praise even if the Sits are not perfect at this stage. *You* are still the one going to the Heel position at this point. Continue working this way until the dog is responding reliably.

Step 4

With the dog sitting at the Heel position, hold the lead in the left hand. Have it unattached from the collar but hanging at the side of the dog's neck. Give the dog the verbal Stay command and the hand signal. Step off on the right foot and walk out the length of the lead. Drop the lead as you go so that it is laying out in front of the dog. This gives your dog the impression that she is still on-lead. Continue walking out until you are about fifteen feet from the dog. Turn and face her, keeping your hands naturally at your sides.

Call your dog by name, and then give the Come command. The dog should come in straight and sit directly in front of you. If you have problems with the dog coming straight to you, set up the plumber's helpers to make a chute. Work within the chute so that the dog is guided in a straight line to you. If she hesitates in coming, or comes in slowly, clap your hands and give some encouragement. Initially, if necessary, make a target for the dog to aim for by kneeling down and spreading your arms out wide. No frowning or criticism! *Make her want to come to you*!

If the dog comes to you without a proper command or anticipates and comes running when you say her name, *don't punish* her. Break off the training. Spend a moment or two playing. Then go on to other training exercises before working on the Recall again.

When the dog is solid on the Recall and comes in to you each time, you have reached the point where you want the *dog* to be the one to finish, the one to go to Heel. Use the dog's name and give the Heel command. Only use extra cues as needed. However, be sure to vary your finishes. *You should be the one to go to Heel at least every fourth time so that the dog does not anticipate the Heel command.*

As you increase the distance on the Recall, use the Plumber's Helpers to make a chute. This will guide the dog directly to you.

Step 5

If the dog continues to respond well, increase the distance another ten feet or so. Once the dog has successfully reached this point, it is time to gradually increase the distance you go away until your dog is coming on a Recall of thirty feet. Train your dog at this point until she comes with only one command.

Once the dog is doing the Recall at thirty feet off-lead, vary the distances. Go closer as well as farther away so that the dog stays sharp. You don't want her to begin stopping in the middle of the Recall or begin to overshoot the mark.

At these longer distances, problems may arise. If the dog consistently comes in slowly, put the lead back on and use the Chase Recall to help spark performance.

CHASE RECALL

The Chase Recall really gets the sluggish dog moving. With the dog sitting on-lead at the Heel position, give the Stay command. Starting on your right foot, go out to the full length of the lead. Say the dog's name, and as you give the Come command, turn with the lead in your left hand and run away from the dog to a distance of about six feet. As you run, look back and encourage your dog to follow along. As the dog runs along behind you, stop, turn around, face her and guide her in to you with as straight a Sit as possible. If the dog overshoots you when you stop, quickly back up a few more paces so she winds up sitting in front of you.

As she is coming toward you, use the bubble if necessary to get a Sit. Repeat the Chase Recall several times in a row to get the dog a little more fired up and enthusiastic.

CHRONIC CROOKED SITS

If you are having trouble with the dog coming in crooked, you can straighten out the problem with the following simple training aid.

The V Funnel

Use two boards approximately two inches wide and two to four feet long. Place them on edge in a V shape. At the narrow end, leave a space wide enough so that you can step through. Stand at the wide end. As you call the dog to you, go backward. Start at the wide end of the boards and back out the narrow end. The dog is funnelled directly in front of you into a straight sit.

THE DOG REFUSES TO COME ON RECALL

This training aid is designed for the dog who refuses to come on recall or stops along the way to you.

Correction from a Distance

You will need someone to help you in order to use this training aid. Use it if you have a problem with the dog refusing to come to you as you go out the longer distances, or if she will only come in partway. Attach a thirty-foot monofilament fishing line to a very lightweight snap swivel.

Lay the line out straight in the training area. Then stand next to the dog at the Heel position. Attach the line to the live ring of the collar as unobtrusively as you can. You want to make as little of the movement of attaching the line as possible.

Station your helper at the other end of the line. Give the dog the command Sit/Stay. Go out whatever distance you choose, and turn and face the dog. Your assistant is now behind you holding the end of the line. Using the dog's name, give the Come command.

If the dog doesn't move, your assistant pulls straight back on the line with a good, firm pull. The dog doesn't know where the correction is coming from. You are just standing there with your arms relaxed at your sides. The dog usually will decide that it is possible to get a correction even while not on-lead, so she had better head straight for you! As she takes off and comes toward you, encourage with lots of enthusiastic words in order to keep the dog coming the full distance.

If the dog comes in partway and stops, your assistant must be alert enough to reel in the line as the dog comes toward you, and quick enough to give another correction when the dog stops.

Some dogs are sensitive to the weight of the snap swivel and fishing line training aid. When it is on their collar they will come on Recall without the correction from your assistant. However, if you then remove it, they do not come on Recall. For this problem there is a different solution.

This time don't use a snap swivel at all. Tie a heavy thread, buttonhole thread for instance, to the live ring of the collar. Lay it out just like the fishing line. You give the Sit/Stay command and move out. When you turn and give the Come command and get no reaction from the dog, your assistant yanks the thread and gets one firm correction in when needed. The thread will probably snap, but the dog will feel enough of a correction to get moving.

Because the thread is almost weightless, your dog won't know whether or not it is in place. The element of surprise in the correction is what will work here. Each time you use this method, you will have to retie the thread on the collar, of course. In any case, you can't use this correction too many times, or the element of surprise is taken away.

If the dog is really reluctant to do the Recall, put the lead back on and start at the beginning. You will also have to think about your training technique to see if you are doing something that is causing problems.

HANDLER CUES

Since the Recall is a complex exercise, handlers sometimes fall into bad habits that are costly in the show ring. Cues are considered *second commands*, or handler error, and these are not allowed in the ring. Most handlers don't even realize they are using body language to cue the dog. A few of the more common ones include curling the toes up as you face the dog to give the command Come. Some handlers bow slightly when they call the dog. On the Finish, some dip their knees slightly or flick their wrists backward as the dog goes to Heel. *None of these cues are allowed in the show ring*, so be very aware of what you are doing. Dogs love body cues. They frequently will respond to the smallest of these cues and turn a deaf ear to a verbal command. Try to relax as you work and eliminate any fidgets or slight movements that can be interpreted by the dog (or the judge) as second commands.

STAND FOR EXAMINATION OFF-LEAD

Earlier in training, your dog was introduced to the Stand for Examination on-lead. Now that she is Heeling off-lead, the exercise must be modified so that it can be performed off-lead as called for in Obedience Trials.

Teaching the Exercise

Heel the dog for a few paces off-lead, then stop, giving a Stand command. At the same time, turn toward the dog, stoop down and with your left hand, palm downward, fingers together, lightly touch the front of the dog's right rear leg, barely brushing her underside. Stand back up and pause for several seconds. If she moves or attempts to sit down, correct with an "ah-ah."

Give your dog a verbal Stay command accompanied by a Stay hand signal. At first, move out from the dog only a short distance. Gradually increase the distance to approximately six feet. Turn and face your dog. An assistant should approach and examine the dog. Have the assistant present the back of his or her hand to the dog to sniff. Then he or she touches the dog's head, back and hindquarters. The dog should remain motionless and not display any shyness or timidity during the examination. Once the assistant has completed the examination and moved away from the dog, count off a few seconds, and then return, walking around in back of the dog to the Heel position. Hold her at the Stand position for a second or two. Then say the dog's name, give a Heel command, take two steps forward and Halt.

If you have any difficulty with any phase of this exercise, put the dog back on-lead to correct the problem you encounter.

When introducing the Heel hand signal, make a scooping movement turning your palm from back to front. As you step off on the left foot, your leg gives the lead a tug that gets the dog moving with you.

9

Early Introduction to Hand Signals

TEACHING YOUR DOG the hand signals this early in training will put in place building blocks that will work for you and your dog right through Utility exercises. It will increase a dog's attention span and ability to focus, since he now will learn to be alert to your movements as well as your voice.

If you do not plan to take your dog beyond the Novice exercises, you may still find it interesting to teach these hand signals. They can be very useful in daily activities with your dog. Even though at this stage hand signals will not replace voice command they will make him more attentive to your commands. The challenge of learning something new will keep the dog interested in training.

When teaching and using these hand signals, be careful to use your hands and arms correctly. Remember that your dog has a different perspective than you do. He is looking up at you. Keep your movements slow and smooth. Be sure that the angle at which you hold your hands makes the signal clear to the dog. Don't give the dog a view of only your fingertips and expect him to be able to interpret the hand signal correctly.

Your dog has already been taught the Sit/Stay and the Down/ Stay. What will be introduced here is the Moving Stand and Stay, as well as the Heel, Down, Sit, Come and Finish hand signals.

Initially, each hand signal should be taught as a separate exercise. Introduce them gradually. The Heel hand signal is one of the easier ones to teach, so start with that. When the dog understands this hand signal, move along to the others. By working this way, you will have the advantage of teaching the dog to be alert to commands that are physical as well as verbal.

During training, after the hand signal is executed and the handler returns to the dog, I recommend that the handler then pause, give a Heel command, take two steps forward and halt. This is an important step to include in training. You don't want the dog anticipating commands.

HEEL HAND SIGNAL

Have the dog sit beside you in the Heel position. Hold the lead in your right hand. Pick up any slack in the lead and fold it into your right palm. You want the lead to lay across the top of your legs with just enough slack so that you are not tugging at the dog's collar.

Say the dog's name, give the Heel command *verbally* and start off on your left foot. *At the same time, move your left arm away from your body, fingers together, palm facing the dog.* Your hand will move to the far side of the dog's head. Keep your hand forward of his eyes so he can see what you are doing. If you have a small dog, do not stoop or bend over to give the hand signal. It is not necessary. The dog will sense the motion of your hand and see it in peripheral vision as it comes forward. Move your hand across in front of the dog with a small, scooping movement, turning your palm toward the front with a sweeping movement forward. Keep the movement slow and smooth so the dog can follow what your are doing with your hand. Exaggerate the movement at first until the dog becomes familiar with it.

As you step forward on your left foot, the lead will be pulled forward by your leg and the dog will move along with you without any need to correct. Once the dog is moving forward, make a few turns and halt.

Once the dog responds reliably when given the hand signal Heel while working on-lead, begin working off-lead. Use the verbal command and hand signal, then gradually change over to the hand signal alone.

110

STAND HAND SIGNAL

This hand signal can be introduced on or off-lead. The Stand hand signal is given while the dog is heeling at a normal pace. It is used in competition for the Signal Exercise and the Moving Stand and Examination required in Utility work.

To practice this hand signal, heel your dog at a normal pace. Give the command Stand and then give the Stay hand signal. As you say *"Stand," sweep your right hand away from the dog's face.* As you say *"Stay," sweep your right hand back toward the dog's face.* Keep your fingers together, palm toward the dog. Stop a few inches in front of his face. Make the movement slow and smooth so it does not seem menacing or hostile to the dog. Initially, you may turn slightly and block the dog's movement as you give the Stand command. However, phase that movement out of your training as soon as possible. In competition you cannot use your body to block the dog's movements either by stepping in front of him or leaning over.

If, at the start, the dog does not stop moving when given the Stand command and hand signal, you can also lightly touch the dog's flank with the edge of your left hand as you did when teaching the basic Novice Stand. Then move your right hand back toward his face in the Stay hand signal.

After the dog does Stands and Stays, you continue walking a few steps further. Be sure you move off on your right foot so that he is given the extra cue to remain in place. Then turn and face the dog. Do not look directly at him. After ten or fifteen seconds, you return to the dog, going around to the Heel position.

As the dog becomes steady, increase the distance you go out to between ten and fifteen feet. Vary how long you stand and face the dog from between fifteen and thirty seconds.

DOWN HAND SIGNAL

When you are ready for a real challenge, try the Down hand signal. You are given the choice of using a verbal command or hand signal in Open training for the Drop on Recall, but in the Signal Exercise in Utility, it is required.

With the dog on-lead in the Heel position, give the Sit command. Hold the lead in your left hand. Step off on your right foot to cue the dog to remain in place. Walk forward a few steps and turn and face

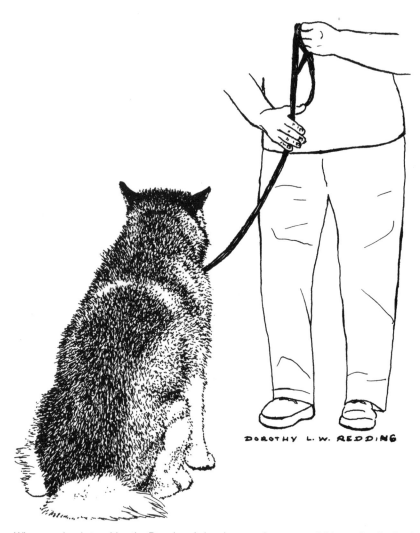

When you *begin* teaching the Drop hand signal, as you lower your right arm slap the lead with a downward motion to give the idea you want the dog to go down.

the dog. Fold up any extra lead. You only want enough lead so that it is slightly taut but not pulling at the dog's collar.

Extend your right arm out to the side at shoulder height, and raise your hand as though stopping traffic. Keep your fingers together, palm facing forward. Then drop your hand to your side and give the verbal command Down. When you begin teaching this hand signal, slap the lead with a downward motion of the right hand as you lower it. Hitting

112

the lead in this manner gives the dog the idea that you want him to go down. Use this training aid until the dog knows what he is expected to do. Once the command and hand signal are understood, you can eliminate hitting the lead.

Just a caution about this hand signal. When you give it in competition, you cannot keep your hand raised too long. Practice by raising your arm from your side as you count a-thousand-and-one. Next, hold your hand up for the count of a-thousand-and-two. Finally, let your hand drop to your side as you count a-thousand-and-three. This method of counting will give you the correct timing. Vary the time that you keep the dog in the Down position from five to twenty seconds. Then return and go around the dog to the Heel position.

As you advance, put the dog on a Sit/Stay off-lead. Starting on your right foot, walk away from the dog to a distance of five to ten feet. Turn and face the dog. Pause. Then give the Down command and hand signal. This time, however, you will add an extra cue the first few times you work off-lead. As you raise your hand, make a fist. Once your hand is fully raised, open your fist. The extra motion reinforces the command. Then drop you arm back to your side. Eliminate this cue as soon as the dog is going down readily.

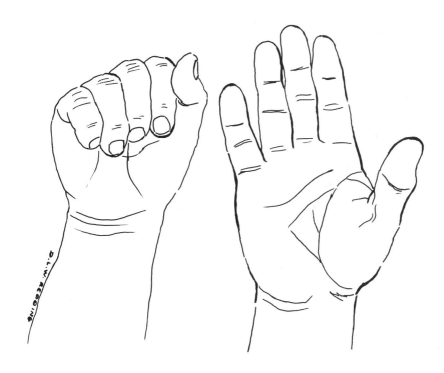

If the dog does not go down, take a step or two toward him, bend down slightly and give a firm verbal command and hand signal. Put a little authority in your voice. Once your dog goes down, give a word of praise and step back to your original position. Vary the time you keep the dog in the Down position. Then return to the dog and go to the Heel position.

Once the dog drops reliably from the Sit position, begin the exercise by walking the dog into a Stand/Stay. Practice the exercise from a Stand position in the same way as you did from the sitting position.

SIT HAND SIGNAL

The Sit hand signal brings the dog up from a Down position into a Sit. You want the dog to sit up briskly, without edging up in stages or creeping forward. It is used in the Utility Signal Exercises.

With the dog at your side in the Heel position, give the Down and Stay commands. Hold the lead in your right hand and, starting on your right foot, walk forward about three feet. Turn and face the dog. Take up any excess lead and fold it into your palm so that there is very little slack. Hold the lead at waist level. Pause for a few seconds.

Then move your left arm about a foot away from the side of your body. Your palm is facing to the back, hand relaxed and fingers together. As you give the verbal Sit command, twist your wrist so that the flat of your palm turns and faces the dog. Give your hand enough of a flip that you catch the dog's attention. Continue moving your left hand up and under the lead. Lift it upward smartly with the edge of your palm.

If this pull on the lead is not sufficient to bring the dog up to a sitting position, pull the lead that you are holding in your right hand downward as well. Simply let it slide over the edge of the left hand like a pulley. Keep the lead high enough so the lead is pulled upward, not forward. Once the dog sits, drop your left hand back to your side. When the dog understands the verbal and hand command and sits smartly, eliminate pulling on the lead. Once the dog is sitting, return around your dog to the Heel position.

As you see further improvement, eliminate the verbal command. Finally, when the dog is ready, begin working off-lead. At that point, extend the distance that you move away from the dog *gradually* until you reach approximately five to ten feet. *Remember, you always have*

To bring the dog up into the Sit position, give the Sit hand signal. Then continue moving your hand up and under the lead. Lift it upward smartly. If necessary, pull the lead in your right hand downward at the same time.

greater control when you work close to the dog. Do not go out thirty or forty feet in the early stages of teaching this hand signal.

When you give the hand signal, be sure to rotate your hand with a little snap so that you get the dog's attention. Also, remember the dog's point of view and, as you turn your palm toward the dog, be sure to present it to him fully. You want the dog to see a good signal. Don't show just the tips of your fingers.

COME HAND SIGNAL

As the name implies, this hand signal teaches the dog to come to you. Initially, you use the verbal *and* hand commands. Eventually, the dog will come to you with only the hand signal. It may be used in Open work for the Come on Recall and is used in Utility for the Signal Exercises. It also gives you an alternate method to call your dog to you under everyday circumstances.

Sit your dog at your side. Give the Stay command and hand signal. Holding the lead in your left hand and starting off on your right foot, walk out about two-thirds the length of the lead and turn and face your dog. Hold the lead at waist height.

Extend your right arm straight out to the side, at shoulder height, palm facing forward. As you give the verbal Come command, bring your right hand back to the center of your chest. Move your hand slowly and smoothly. Make it a sweeping gesture. Feel as though you are pulling as much air as you can toward you with your arm. Do not, however, keep your arm extended for a prolonged period of time. Use the counting method as you did for the Down hand signal.

Keep the lead high enough with the left hand so that you can slap it smartly with your right hand as it sweeps toward your chest. This will give the dog a tug that will bring him toward you. As he begins to understand what you want, and comes to you on command, eliminate hitting the lead. Once the dog is sitting in front of you for five to ten seconds, return around the dog to the Heel position.

In the next step, work off-lead. Put the dog on a Sit/Stay. Starting on the right foot, walk out five to ten feet, turn and face the dog. Pause. Since you are now working off-lead, use the verbal command and the Come hand signal at this point. *Gradually* phase out the verbal command.

Once you give the Come hand signal, the dog must come quickly. Keep your hand movement broad and sweeping. If your dog pauses or starts to slow up, encourage him verbally and also by clapping your hands. Try taking a step or two backward. The movement will help to keep the dog coming toward you.

When the dog sits in front of you, be sure he sits squarely. Alternate between going to Heel yourself and having the dog go to Heel.

FINISH HAND SIGNAL

The Finish hand signal brings the dog to the Heel position, no matter which method of Finish you have taught your dog—the Go-Around or the Swing Finish.

Heel along with the dog on-lead, keeping the lead in the right hand. Without stopping, quickly back up a few steps. Use the dog's name and give a verbal Come command. Once the dog has come to you and is sitting squarely in front of you, pause for a moment or two. Then give the hand signal Finish.

The hand signal is a simple twist of the wrist. With your fingers together, and your palm facing backward, make a scooping, circular motion around to the front. Then drop your arm back to your side in a relaxed manner. Use the right hand for the go-around finish and the left hand for the Swing (or Poodle) finish. This brings the dog to your side at the Heel position. Remember, during training, once the dog is sitting in the Heel position, give a Heel command, take two steps forward and Halt.

Next, Heel along with the dog off-lead. Then take several steps backward, use the dog's name and give the Come command. When the dog sits in front of you, pause and then give a verbal command and hand signal Heel. *As soon as the dog understands the hand signal, drop the verbal command.* Unless the dog is easily distracted or inattentive, teaching this hand signal rarely presents a problem.

REMEMBER TO PRAISE

Although I have not mentioned it after each one of these hand signal exercises, *be sure to praise the dog as you work*. Even if your dog's response is far from perfect when you begin, encourage him. Remember that these are advanced exercises and any progress should meet with your praise and approval. This attitude will build the dog's confidence in his ability to meet training challenges.

Open Training

Never forget your dog is working hard to please you.

10

Moving Successfully into Advanced Training

WHEN YOU BEGIN the work in the Open class, it is understood that your dog is able to perform all of the Novice exercises with agility, confidence and style. Minor problems may still show up, but, overall, the dog's capabilities should be such that she has been able to earn a CD title.

If you have not competed in AKC Novice competition, but feel you still are interested in training your dog in Open work for your own enjoyment, review all of the Novice exercises. Evaluate the dog's performance. If she is able to do all of the Novice exercises proficiently, then you are ready for more advanced work.

Straighten out rough spots now. Don't think small problems will go away as you continue into Open work. They will not. They will cause you further problems. *The dog's building block work must be solidly in place, and all Novice work extremely reliable, before you consider Open work.*

WHAT IS EXPECTED

In Open work, the exercises are complex, with components that are based upon things learned in Novice training. However, as you go forward, a greater degree of precision and concentration is expected of both the dog and the handler. The attention span of the dog must be built up throughout this training period. The dog's concentration must become focused enough, so that by the time she has finished Open training, no distraction interferes with performance.

The handler must also be alert so as not to accommodate the dog at any time. The handler's footwork and body postures should become smoother and more polished. Additional ''cues'' for the dog are to be eliminated. The commands, even under stress, must be given in clear, pleasant tones. The handler has the responsibility of being focused and in control at all times.

WHY ARE WE DOING THIS!

Remember to praise your dog enthusiastically. She's working hard to please you. Don't ever forget that!

Sometimes, handlers get frustrated or overeager, and they forget that the dog is doing the best she can. *Keep a sense of humor* and keep your perspective. *There is no place for anger in training.* Keep your voice under control. Break off training for a few minutes if you start seriously losing your patience. Be sure you are making what you want clear to the dog. She has an entirely different perspective on things than you do. Sometimes, strangely enough, this concept comes as a big surprise to handlers.

IT'S BEEN SAID BEFORE

I want to repeat something here that I have very strong feelings about. Earlier in the book, I made my position clear on food as reward and reinforcement. I repeat it here for emphasis. Food rewards are not the way to get a dog to work reliably. *Praise and affection will mean more to your dog than any bit of food.* Letting your dog know that what she is doing is very pleasing to you will encourage her to work from the heart and will bring out the best the dog has to offer. Experiencing this kind of loyalty and love from your dog is one of the happier experiences in life.

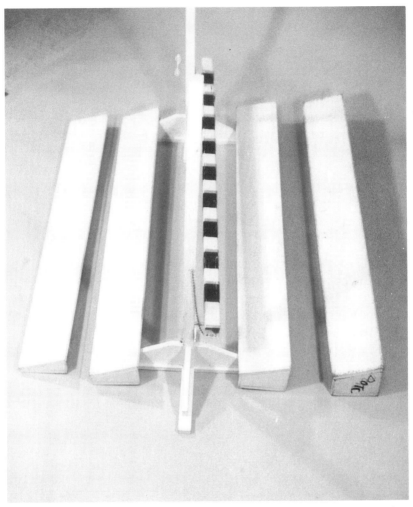

Equipment: The Broad Jump, Solid Jump and Utility Bar Jump are needed to introduce jumping work.

EQUIPMENT

When you are ready for Open work, you will need a set of practice High Jumps and Broad Jumps, plus the Utility bar. Light weight plastic sets are available. They are convenient to carry if you need to travel to your training site. However, if you are interested in making your own set, you will find suggestions for construction in Appendix A.

In addition to the jumps, if you will be working on a hard, smooth or slick surface, it is recommended that you use rubber runners in the areas where the dog starts the jump and where he lands to prevent slipping and possible injury. If you train outdoors on grass, mats will not be necessary.

You will also need several wooden or plastic dumbbells of an appropriate size for your dog. Information and selecting and fitting the dumbbell is found in Chapter Eleven.

Additional training aids that are extremely useful in Open work are plumber's helpers and a twenty-foot lead made of lightweight rope (such as window sash cord) with a lightweight snap swivel attached. A dowel bar is also useful in jump training.

The Dowel Bar

To make a dowel bar, use a one-half-inch to one-inch diameter wooden bar or dowel that is three or four feet long. Drill a hole in each end. Cut two eight-inch to ten-inch pieces from a metal clothes hanger. Bend two inches of the wire, one each to form an L shape. Insert the short ends of the wire into the holes at the end of the dowel or bar.

Drill two holes on either side of the number two Broad Jump board so that the dowel is centered when the long ends of the wire are inserted into the holes. Paint the dowel a flat white with black stripes every three inches, or use black tape to make the stripes.

This valuable aid can be used during training to help the dog improve jumping ability and technique.

HEELING IN OPEN WORK

Review your on-lead Heeling to be sure the dog is able to perform without lagging, forging, going wide or crowding.

Heel at a normal pace as well as fast and slow. Do Right and Left Turns and the About-Turn and Halt. Give every variety of movement the dog has been trained to perform and vary it enough to hold her attention. Work at a brisk pace that feels good and looks good! That way, the dog must pay attention to keep up with you.

Don't walk endlessly in one direction before you turn. Take a Right Turn and a couple of steps, then a Left Turn and a couple of steps. Do an About-Turn and then go back to straight Heeling. Remember to keep the pace up. And if you really want to get your dog's attention, Halt when you are doing fast Heeling.

OPEN HEELING PATTERN

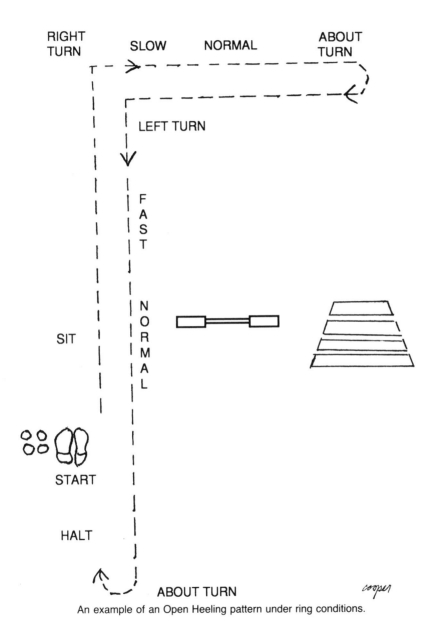

An example of an Open Heeling pattern under ring conditions.

In clinics I have given over the years, I would tell people to warm up their dogs for two full minutes. Very few worked for one full minute, let alone the two allotted. Many were not concentrating on the warm-up. They were lagging themselves. They lost their concentration with the dog. They got careless with their foot work and general handling. Their commands went flat.

Throughout Open work, pay attention to your Heeling, and work the dog both on and off-lead.

In off-lead Heeling, the training is virtually identical to what has been outlined above. There is a difference, however. *When Heeling off-lead, you must count heavily on the dog's reliability.* You only have verbal corrections to work with. For this reason, it is important to first master Heeling on-lead. But as you progress, no matter how long you have been Heeling off-lead, don't be reluctant to go back on-lead if you run into problems. Remember, training always has some ups and downs—that's what makes it a challenge!

ADVANCED FIGURE-EIGHT EXERCISE

In Open training, you are expected to execute the Figure Eight with more precision. When you compete at this more advanced level, you must expect your performance to be viewed with greater scrutiny.

Every movement the handler makes is critical to the dog's performance in this exercise. Be aware of your footwork. Keep your feet low to the ground and out of the dog's way.

As you practice the Figure Eight, keep your Heeling pace steady. Only the dog will speed up around the outside and slow down on the inside curves. When doing this exercise, always remember to place your left foot down last when you halt. *Never forget that your left leg guides the dog.*

Work the Figure Eight both on-lead and off-lead. Go back on-lead any time you are not satisfied. It is not a step backward. Consider it another training method that is most helpful when used intermittently throughout Open and Utility work. If the dog is accustomed to working on and off-lead, it does not seem like a punishment to him if you use the lead as a guide when introducing some of the more advanced exercises.

LONG SIT AND LONG DOWN

These exercises are done in exactly the same manner as the Novice Sit and Down exercises. The difference is that the handler *is out of sight* for a specified period of time. In Open competition on the Long Sit, from the time you leave, you are out of sight for about three minutes. For the Long Down, the period of time is five minutes more or less from the time the judge tells you to leave your dog until told to return to your dog.

Build up the dog's ability to remain focused. Each time you practice, do each of these exercises three to five times. You want to gradually build up your dog's confidence in the fact that, though out of sight, you will return, and that she is to remain in position no matter what the distraction.

Practicing this exercise can be a bit boring at times, but don't brush it off. It is important. If not done well, it can cost you a substantial number of points, or in the extreme case, a score of zero.

Long Sit

Begin your training by practicing the Long Sit as you did in Novice. Don't rush through the exercise. Build up your time slowly. Initially, don't go out of sight.

Sit the dog at your side at the Heel position. Give both the verbal and hand signal Stay. Pause for a moment. Then step off on your right foot, and go out between twenty-five and thirty-five feet. Turn and face the dog without looking directly at her.

Gradually increase the time that you stand facing the dog from one minute to three minutes. Return and go around behind your dog and into the Heel position. Pause briefly, then using the dog's name, give the Heel command, take two steps forward and halt.

In the Obedience ring, when the judge tells you to return to your dog, do so, but *do not add* the Heel command and the extra two steps. That is only used during training to add an element of control for the handler.

When the dog remains in place for three minutes with you in sight, it is time to move out of sight. Select a training area that has a barrier that you can stand behind, out of sight of the dog. If your arrangement is such that you cannot see the dog, have an assistant stand and watch to see if the dog breaks the command. Decide beforehand whether you or your assistant will give the correction should it be necessary.

Start by going out of sight and returning almost immediately. This will get the dog used to the idea that she will lose sight of you. Your quick return does not give the dog time to start craning her neck or moving out of place to look for you.

Increase the time that you are out of sight gradually until you reach a minute and a half. If the dog attempts to get up when you come back into sight, give a firm Sit/Stay command. She'll soon get the idea that no matter how nice it is to see you return, she is to remain in position.

If the dog remains calm and steady at a minute and a half, gradually increase the time to between four and five minutes. Although you need only remain out of sight three minutes for this exercise, it takes time for all of the handlers to exit and return to the ring. For that reason, it is good practice to have the dog sit as long as four or five minutes. She will get used to sitting that long and will not begin to fidget at the end of three minutes.

Long Down

This exercise is taught in exactly the same way as the Long Sit. Before you leave your dog on the Down/Stay, be sure she is lying in a straight line. Do not allow the dog's body to curl to the left or the right. Your dog should be lying at attention throughout the exercise.

Gradually increase the time you stand facing the dog for five minutes before you start going out of sight. Once you reach the point at which you go out of sight, increase the time out of sight gradually from five to seven minutes.

DROP ON RECALL

The Drop on Recall is a combination exercise—actually two Recalls and a Down. It uses the Down taught as early as KPT and the Recall taught during Novice training.

In the Drop on Recall, the dog must come in on the Recall approximately thirty-five feet and Drop on command at any point along the way that the judge selects. The dog is required to drop down immediately and remain down without creeping forward or breaking the position, until the second command Come is given. The dog should then return briskly and sit squarely in front of the handler. On command, the dog goes to the Heel position.

The two most common problems that arise when teaching this exercise are the dog's anticipation of the Down command and sloppy

Recall work. When the dog anticipates the command, she slows down or stops altogether on the way to the handler. The dog is waiting for the command she knows is coming. Vary the distance at which you give the command in order to avoid this problem.

Sloppy Recall work can mean that the dog breaks the Down command and returns to the handler before being given the Come command, or possibly that the dog comes in partway and then stops.

To forestall this kind of response to the exercise, it is practiced in two separate parts—the Drop and the Recall, and then combined when the dog is doing each of them in a consistently steady manner.

What is different about the Down command in training for the Drop On Recall is that the dog is given the command while moving. You want to introduce the concept of going Down as she is in motion.

It is also good to sharpen your dog's Recall work. Practice to be sure that your dog comes to you quickly and in a straight line. If this exercise has been a problem for your dog at the Novice level, drill to improve the dog's performance. By preparing this way, you will have eliminated a serious problem when you are trying to combine the two elements that make up the Drop on Recall.

When you begin teaching the Drop on Recall, use both a verbal command and a hand signal. Pay close attention to your dog's response. Then judge which gets a better reaction from you dog. Some react more quickly to the hand signal, others give a better performance with verbal commands.

When you do the Drop On Recall in the AKC Obedience Trials, you are allowed only one command, either a verbal Down *or* a hand signal. The choice is yours, so be alert to which gets the best reaction from your dog.

When you give the hand signal, raise your right arm at the elbow, palm toward the dog. Keep your elbow out and away from your body. Have your fist closed loosely. Then as you bring your hand down, open the fist as though you were throwing a handful of sand. By making that movement—going from the closed to the open hand—you capture the dog's attention. It may seem like a small movement, but dogs respond well to sight cues.

Teaching the Exercise

Step 1

You are introducing the Down command for the first time while the dog is in motion. There is no Recall or Finish as yet.

You will have to decide how you want to hold your lead. If you use your left hand only, your right hand is free to give the hand signal. If you prefer to hold the lead in both hands, you'll have to practice smoothly switching it to the left hand at the appropriate moment. This choice requires greater coordination to stay in control.

With the dog on-lead, Heel in a straight line. As you are moving, say your dog's name and give the Down command and hand signal at the same time. Since the dog is already familiar with the Down command, with a little practice she should respond quickly.

Vary how far forward you walk before giving the command. Even at this early stage, it is important that the dog not anticipate at what point the command will be given. Be sure that you praise and encourage the dog when she gets it right.

Step 2

Now that the dog goes down while moving, a Recall from the end of the lead is added. While Heeling the dog on-lead in a straight line forward, step back quickly so that the dog turns with you. When the dog starts toward you, continue backing up to the end of the lead, use the dog's name and give the Down command and the hand signal together. Be sure you move your hand smoothly. Let your arm go straight down in one sweeping motion to your side.

If the dog hesitates, or does not go down at all, pull down on the lead to communicate the idea that the dog is to go down immediately. Once the dog is down, praise quickly. Then count off a few seconds. Vary how long the dog is down so that she does not anticipate the next command. Then give the command Come. The dog has only a short distance to come to you, but should do so quickly and sit squarely in front of you.

Vary the finish. Have the dog go to Heel *or* you go around behind the dog into the Heel position yourself. Then give the Heel command, take two steps forward and halt. Praise your dog's efforts.

Step 3

Now you start working off-lead. Again, heel the dog forward and then step backward as you did in the previous step, except without the lead.

Give the Come command. As the dog comes toward you, back up further. Then give the Down command *and* hand signal together. Praise the dog *quietly* when she goes down. You don't want her bobbing up. When your dog is slow in responding, correct with a tone of authority.

Once she is down, wait for a few seconds. *It is essential to vary the length of time.* Then give the Come command. The dog knows the Recall and should come to you in a straight line and sit directly in front of you. Vary the finish as before.

Step 4

Now that the dog is accustomed to going down while moving, you perform the exercise as you will be doing it in competition.

In this step, however, you go out from the dog only for a distance of fifteen feet. Working a little closer enables you to correct more quickly, if it is necessary.

Have the dog sit at your left side. Give the Stay command and hand signal. Step off on the right foot and go forward approximately ten to fifteen feet. Turn and face the dog. Do not look directly at her.

Stand with your arms relaxed at your sides. Even in practice, be careful not to develop little second-command body cues. Wait for a few seconds and then give the verbal command Come.

Let the dog come toward you for a few paces and then give both the verbal Down command *and* the hand signal together. The dog is not quite ready for only one command as yet. If correction is needed, go back to the dog and give another verbal Down command and hand signal. Put a little authority into the tone of your voice, but don't sound angry. You just want the dog to know that you're not pleased and that you expect her to do better.

Remember, this is basically a Recall exercise. *You want the dog to come to you enthusiastically. Don't use corrections that will cause the dog to shy away from you. Encouragement and praise work better.* When necessary, an authoritative voice should be all that you need to get your point across.

Once the dog is down successfully, pause before calling her to you. Don't let the dog anticipate. Use her name and give the Come command. You use the dog's name to get attention. However, the dog *must* begin moving *only* on the Come command. Once the command is given, be sure she comes in quickly and sits squarely. Vary the finish.

Step 5

Sit the dog and give the Stay command and hand signal. Go out approximately thirty-five feet. Turn and face the dog. Wait a few seconds and then give the dog the command Come. As the dog comes toward you, give the verbal Down command *and* hand signal together. Use both until the dog is reliable and goes down on command each time. Then choose one or the other and work from then on with either the verbal command or the hand signal, but not both. Remember, you will only be able to use *one* in competition.

Remember to vary the amount of time the dog is kept down before you give the Come command. The dog has learned that she must pay attention and be alert throughout this exercise. Your dog will stay alert if you challenge her and vary both your timing and the place where you give the dog the command to go down. Give the Down command when she has come only a few paces toward you *or* wait until she is almost in front of you. Don't forget to give plenty of praise.

If the dog begins to slow down before dropping on command, go back to straight Recalls. This is anticipating. If you continue to have problems, go back on-lead. You might also examine your own performance to be sure it is not handler error or unintentional training that is causing the problem.

It is helpful, in order to prevent the dog from anticipating the Drop on Recall, to intersperse this exercise with a straight Recall. Do several straight Recalls for each Drop on Recall practiced.

11

Selecting and Working with the Dumbbell

IN CHOOSING a properly fitted dumbbell for your dog, you must consider the diameter and the length of the shaft, the height and shape of the bells and the overall weight.

The proper diameter of the shaft of a dumbbell has always been a difficult problem. There doesn't seem to be a measurement technique that is wholly reliable. I recommend that the shaft should be of a size that fits in the dog's mouth firmly behind the canines without rolling around. The fit should be snug. If, in selecting the proper shaft size, there is any doubt, go with the slightly larger size. In addition, you want it long enough so that the end bells do not obstruct the dog's view.

The bell height determines how high up off the ground the shaft will be when the dog picks it up. Many dogs, particularly the shorter muzzled dogs, pick up the dumbbell from the top, even if there is enough of a gap underneath to scoop it up. Others, if the gap is sufficient, choose to pick it up from underneath.

Once you have an estimate of the size of the bells, their shape must be considered.

Square bells (ends) tend to obscure the dog's vision and add weight. As a result I prefer an octagonal or a wedged-shaped dumbbell.

Two examples of well-fitted dumbbells. They are balanced and in proper proportion to the size of the dog. The bells do not obstruct the dog's vision.

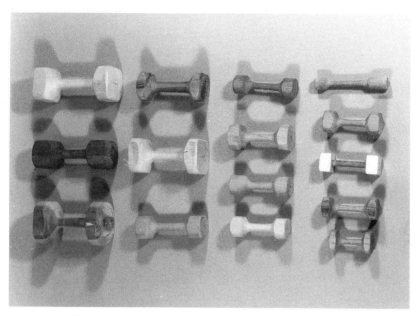

There is enough variety in dumbbells to fit any dog properly.

There is a wide range of shapes and sizes that are available. If you are handy, you can make your own.

The length of the shaft must also be considered. The shaft should be sufficiently wide so that the bells do not press against the lips. In breeds with face hair, such as the Miniature Schnauzer, you may want to allow slightly more. But don't overdo it. The shaft should never be so long that the dog can pick the dumbbell up off-center and have it dangle while carrying it.

The best test is simply to place the dumbbell in the dog's mouth. If it appears balanced and proportional to the size of the dog, and if he can see over the bells, chances are you have made a good choice.

If you order dumbbells from a catalog, before doing so get some different sizes of doweling at the hardware store and see what size seems comfortable in the dog's mouth. Between that and the bell suggestions offered above, you should be able to outfit the dog suitably.

It is also a good idea to purchase several dumbbells. Depending on the color of the surface you will be working on, you may want the bells painted a flat white. You also need to have an extra one in case your dumbbell breaks. Particularly at a show, you must come prepared for any such problems.

Whether you make your own or order them through a catalog, your dumbbells should be made of either plastic or hardwoods such as poplar, ash or maple.

If you start teaching your dog to take the dumbbell when quite young, remember that as a dog grows bigger, he will require a larger dumbbell. If you think this in an obvious point, let me assure you that I've seen handlers using dumbbells that dogs had long outgrown.

THROWING THE DUMBBELL

Hold the dumbbell by the bell with the tips of your thumb and fingers. Rotate your wrist so that the thumb is on the top of the bell. Throw the dumbbell with the right hand so you don't inadvertently hit the dog as you raise your arm.

To toss the dumbbell, fully extend your arm and lock your elbow and wrist. Bring your fully extended arm forward, releasing the dumbbell at approximately shoulder height. Continue a follow-through motion with the arm.

Don't snap your wrist when you throw it or you'll get an undesirable spin. If you are throwing on a hard surface, the spin is more likely to cause one of the bells to hit and bounce or roll. On a grass surface, the dumbbell is more apt to stay where it lands. Needless to say, the bell shape, square or beveled, will also be a factor in how the dumbbell lands.

The Left-Handed Thrower

If you are left-handed, throw the dumbbell in exactly the same manner. However, extra care must be taken not to hit the dog. Many instructors encourage the left hander to learn to throw the dumbbell with the right hand. My own opinion is that you should use whatever hand is comfortable.

In either case, it is important to practice throwing the dumbbell without the dog until you have good control.

RETRIEVE ON THE FLAT

To begin this exercise, the dog sits at the Heel position. The handler gives the dog the Stay command and/or hand signal and then throws the dumbbell straight out approximately twenty feet. On com-

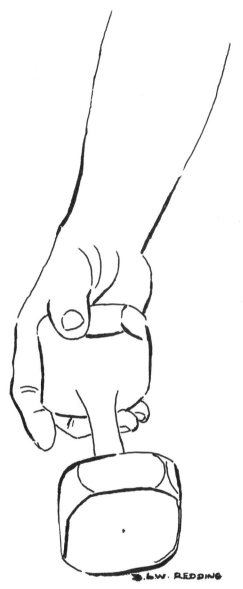

To throw the dumbbell, hold the bell with the tips of your fingers and rotate your wrist so the thumb is on top.

mand, the dog goes directly to the dumbbell, picks it up and returns and to sit squarely in front of the handler. The dog must sit close enough so the handler can take the dumbbell without stretching or stepping forward. How quickly the dog does this is extremely important. The dog then finishes in the same manner as in the Novice Recall.

Teaching the Exercise

This exercise is taught in a series of progressive steps. At first, the dog simply learns to take and give the dumbbell as in KPT. Then he is taught to take it while in motion.

Next, the dog learns to pick the dumbbell up off the ground and give it to the handler.

Finally (starting at a few feet and gradually moving out to approximately twenty feet), the dog goes out, retrieves the dumbbell and brings it back, sitting directly in front of the handler. The handler says "Give," and takes the dumbbell. Then, on command, the dog goes to the Heel position and sits.

In order to go out briskly to retrieve the dumbbell, the dog must be able to follow the movement of the dumbbell when you throw it. Therefore, *how you throw the dumbbell is important.*

Also, when the dog is going out ten to twenty feet, it is easy to become distracted by noises or extraneous activity and lose concentration. Should that occur, you must get out to the dog quickly and redirect his attention to the dumbbell. You then go back to your original position, coax your dog back to you, if necessary, and continue with the exercise.

Teaching the Dog to Take the Dumbbell

Step 1

You begin teaching this exercise using articles similar to the ones that you used in training play in KPT. This was an essential building block that taught the words "take" and "give" as the puppy took toys and dowels from you and gave them back to you.

If your dog did not have the advantage of this kind of play learning, review that section. A few minutes of "play" each day for a week or two will quickly bring the dog to the point of understanding the command words Take and Give and readily responding by accepting and giving back the play articles.

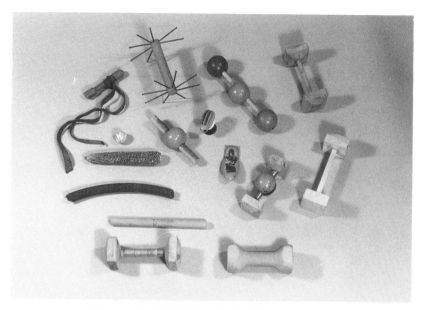

An assortment of training aids for "play learning."

Keep the dog on-lead as you play in order to limit the opportunities to run off with the articles. You will defeat the purpose of this training if the dog can reduce it to a catch-me game. In order to be sure that you do not need to offer any corrections when playing, *you must be in control of how you play the game.* You want to focus on encouragement and praise so that the dog learns to take and give enthusiastically because it pleases you so much when he does so.

Be sure that you only spend a short time playing and that each session ends before the dog loses interest. Once the dog understands the commands, you're ready to start training using the dumbbell.

Step 2

With the dog sitting in front of you, show the dumbbell and say "Take It." When you offer the dumbbell, hold the bell ends in both hands. Make a fist over the bells with the knuckles toward the dog. Keep the shaft clear. This directs the dog to take the dumbbell by the shaft. If your dog takes it on his own, praise enthusiastically.

If he refuses to take the dumbbell, use your middle finger and thumb to take hold of the dog's lower jaw (about two inches back on the average dog) and press the skin against the teeth. Hold the collar in order to control your dog's head.

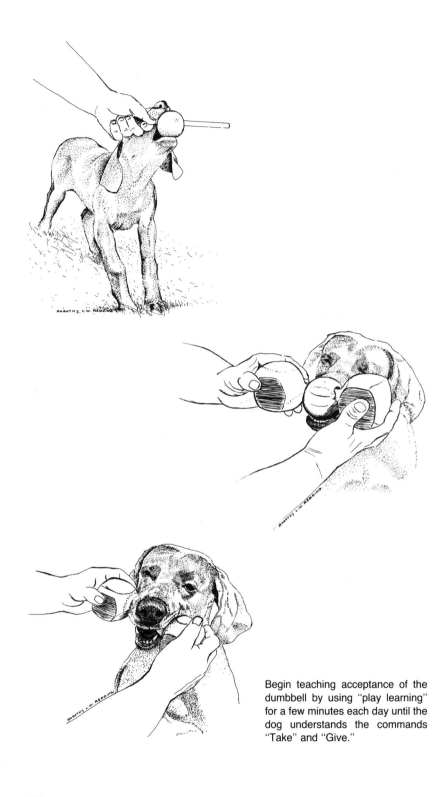

Begin teaching acceptance of the dumbbell by using "play learning" for a few minutes each day until the dog understands the commands "Take" and "Give."

140

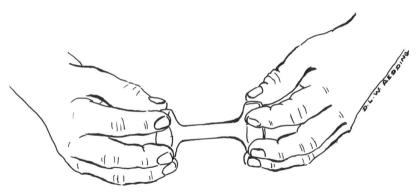

When you offer the dumbbell, keep the shaft clear. Hold the bell ends in both hands, making a fist over the bells with the knuckles toward the dog.

Don't be rough. Don't exert any more pressure than is necessary to get the dog to open his mouth. He isn't sure yet what you want, so do this as calmly and as gently as possible, all the while talking in an encouraging way as you put the dumbbell in his mouth. If necessary, hold the dog's mouth closed around the dumbbell for a few seconds without covering his eyes with your hand. Encourage him again. "What a good dog!" Praise and let him know you are pleased when he takes it.

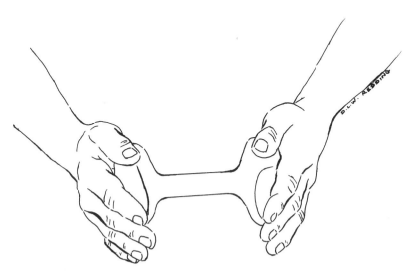

To take the dumbbell from the dog, with the fingers straight out, raise your hands from below the dumbbell and take hold of the bells.

Once your dog takes the dumbbell on his own, and holds it for a few seconds, you want to teach giving back. Raise your hands (fingers straight out) from below the dumbbell, and take hold of the bells with your fingers as you say "Give." As the dog releases the dumbbell, praise him. Let him know that he is doing what you want and is really pleasing you.

If the dog refuses to give up the dumbbell, try giving a tap on one of the bells. That little vibration should help. For a really stubborn dog, use your thumb and middle finger to press in on the lower lip until he lets go. Say "Give." Keep talking pleasantly. Praise when you get it. You're not ready yet for reprimands if he doesn't give it back immediately. *Don't snatch the dumbbell from the dog.* He's still learning. Make sure that you have a happy voice and smile. It should seem like play to him, but realize that you are at a very critical point.

Keep working with the dog once or twice each day until he takes the dumbbell and holds it for several seconds and gives it back to you on command.

It is important that you break off this exercise on a high note if at all possible. Once he has taken the dumbbell and given it back successfully a few times, go on to something else.

Step 3

The purpose of this step is to teach your dog to take the dumbbell while he is in motion. Introduce your dog to this exercise *either* on- or off-lead. If you elect to work off-lead be sure you work the dog in a controlled area. The plumber's helpers can be a great aid here.

Don't use a Heel command. Just walk forward with the dog on your left side. Then, holding the dumbbell in your right hand by the bell, offer it to the the dog. Hold it about a foot or so in front of him and straight across the muzzle. The shaft should be parallel to the floor.

Tell him Take It. You want your dog to reach out and take it from your hand. At first he may turn his head away from the dumbbell. If this is the case, place your fingers through the collar and guide the dog toward the dumbbell. Make it interesting. Move the dumbbell around a bit, but keep the movement slow enough so he can follow it. Tease with it a little to create some interest. If your dog takes the dumbbell, tell him "Good dog." Heel along no more than a step or two further. Don't give the dog time to drop it. Then take it from him. If your dog does drop it, put the dumbbell back in his mouth for a few seconds and then take it. *Don't* give a correction. Break off the exercise and try it again later.

Step 4

By now your dog should be taking the dumbbell from you whether you are just sitting and practicing Take and Give or when he's on-lead and moving. When the dog does this reliably, begin having him take the dumbbell from you at lower heights.

Start by holding the dumbbell at an accustomed height—in front of him at eye level. Have the dog take it and give it back.

Once you are successful with it at eye level, move the dumbbell down between the dog's eye level and the ground. Give the command Take It. Remember to praise as he does so. Next, lower the dumbbell so that it is just an inch or two off the ground and repeat the process. Take your time with all these steps so that the dog is really reliable. When he is, it is time for him to pick the dumbbell up off the ground.

To teach the dog to take a dumbbell off the ground or floor, show it to him and move it about while talking to the dog. *You need to get your dog excited about the dumbbell.* When he is eager to take it, place it on the floor or ground in front of him and give the command Take It. If he moves toward the dumbbell to take it, don't say anything until the dog has picked it up. If you distract a dog too soon, he may not pick it up, or may pick it up and drop it. Wait until your dog is holding it, then praise.

Step 5

You are now at the point where you begin throwing the dumbbell farther. Show the dog the dumbbell and throw it out a distance of two to three feet. Tell him to Take It *while it is in the air.* Dogs love to catch things that are moving. If he goes out before you give the verbal command, do *not* correct.

Your goal at this time is to get your dog to go out in a spirited manner and pick up the dumbbell. Wait until he has picked it up, then step back a few paces and say "Come." Use an upbeat voice to keep the dog's enthusiasm up. When the dog comes to you, don't worry about the Sit. All you're teaching right now is to bring the dumbbell back.

Assuming he has not dropped the dumbbell along the way, stoop down and give your dog the command Give. Bring your hands slowly up under his muzzle, and take the dumbbell by the bells with the tips of your fingers. If he doesn't release the dumbbell right away, apply a small pressure against the lower lip and repeat the Give command. When he releases the dumbbell, praise enthusiastically and spend a moment or two playing.

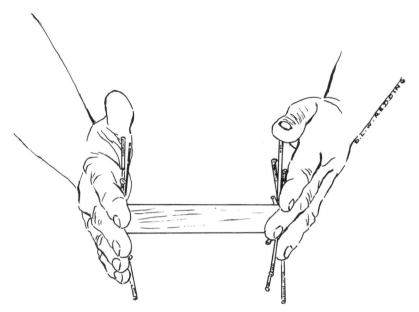

If the dog gets into the habit of picking up the dumbbell by the bell instead of the shaft, drive nails into the end of a piece of dowel. The dog will pick this up by the shaft to avoid the nail heads.

If, on the other hand, your dog does not respond to the Take It command, or moves out slowly, you run out to the dumbbell. Get the dog excited, and moving, make him want to pick it up! When he does, take several steps backward and tell him Come. Don't worry about a perfect Sit, however. Have him give the dumbbell. Use care to keep your hands and fingers away from the dog's eyes. Once you have the dumbbell, praise him!

If the dog brings the dumbbell to you but drops it instead of waiting for you to take it, put it right back in his mouth. If necessary, apply a little pressure on the lower lip to get him to open his mouth. You want to *open the jaws so that you can roll the shaft of the dumbbell behind the canines*. Don't push it too far back where it becomes uncomfortable to hold. He may start mouthing it or try to spit it out. Don't be rough as you do this. Talk to the dog pleasantly. *Don't create resentment*. If he keeps trying to drop it, give a flick of the thumb and forefinger under the chin as you say "Hold it. That's it! Hold it! *Good dog*!"

If the dog habitually picks up the dumbbell by the bell end, there is a training aid that is very useful to break this habit. Take a piece of dowel the same length as your dumbbell and drive nails, like spokes on a wheel, into the dowel on either end. When the dog goes to pick it up during training, he will avoid the nails and pick it up by the shaft.

Once all is going well at two or three feet, increase the distance to between five and ten feet. Take your time here. Don't send the dog out too far, too quickly. Also watch how you correct the dog. Since you want the dog to bring the dumbbell back to you, don't cause him to shy away for fear of punishment. Use no harsh tones or displays of anger, or you will get unreliable performances. Be sure that no matter how firmly you speak to the dog, your voice, facial expression and body language display confidence and authority—not anger.

Progressively increase the distance you throw the dumbbell until you reach twenty to twenty-five feet. Once the dog is retrieving the dumbbell without major problems, begin working on improving the Sit.

Step 6

At this point, you are ready to do the exercise as it would be performed in AKC competition.

Sit the dog at the Heel position, off-lead. Hold the dumbbell in your right hand. Give the dog the verbal Stay command *and* the hand signal with your left hand. Show the dog the dumbbell before throwing it. Make the throw a minimum distance of twenty feet. The dog must not move until given the command.

If the dog consistently breaks and goes out for the dumbbell before given the command, try this training aide. Slide the loop end of the lead through the dog's collar from front to back. Hold the snap swivel in your left hand and hang the loop end on the little finger of your left hand. Fold up the excess lead and hold it. Leave enough hanging down so that it is not taut.

Give the dog the Stay command. Throw the dumbbell out. Pause before giving the command Take It. The lead will remind the dog to stay in place. If necessary, pull back to keep him sitting.

When you give the command Take It, drop the loop off your little finger and let it slide through the dog's collar as he takes off. Be sure to drop the *loop end*, not the snap swivel. You don't want to hit the dog with it. Also, vary the amount of time you pause before giving the command Take It. This technique works well because although it makes a correction, it does so without dampening the dog's enthusiasm.

Given the command, the dog then goes out in a straight line, picks up the dumbbell and returns smartly, sitting squarely in front of the handler.

The dog should sit close enough so you don't have to lean forward or take a step in order to take the dumbbell. He should not be sitting so close, however, as to be touching. Sitting too far or touching are cause for deductions in the Obedience ring.

Count off a second or two, then say "Give." Reach out and take the dumbbell. The dog should release it immediately. Then use the dog's name and give the command Heel. The dog should come to the Heel position and sit there correctly.

When the dog is retrieving at this distance, he may be distracted by some noise or activity and slow down the pace, or come to a complete stop. If this happens, quickly walk toward the dumbbell, pointing to it, and encourage the dog to pick it up.

If he takes it, step back a few steps and let him sit directly in front of you. Then complete the exercise as described above. If he doesn't take it, show that you are displeased by the tone of your voice. Place the dumbbell in his mouth. Firmly give the command Take! Hold! Once he takes it in his mouth, give praise. Take a step or two back and call him. As above, the dog should sit directly in front of you. Give the command Give. Once he gives you the dumbbell, count off a few seconds, then give the command to go to the Heel position. Praise the dog.

Some dogs are slower in learning to take the dumbbell, and some just don't want to give it up once they get it—no matter what!

I remember a seminar that I once gave. They told me before I even went there that they had a Doberman who would latch on to a dumbbell and never let it go. He became rigid when he picked the dumbbell up, absolutely rigid. He wouldn't let go no matter what. I was told that this was the dog of all dogs—the one that would defeat me! "No problem," I said.

When I arrived, they were all waiting for me. It was all very friendly, of course, but nevertheless, they were really waiting to see what I could do.

I brought a special dumbbell that I had made. I had taken metal tubing that fit over the shaft of the dumbbell and cut the tubing into pieces. I fixed the dumbbell so that one end came off. I then slid the tubing piece over the dumbbell shaft and put the bell back on the end of it.

At the beginning of the seminar, I gave the dog a regular dumb-

My "special dumbbell" cure for the dog who latched on to the dumbbell, went rigid and wouldn't let go.

bell. He just stood there with it in his mouth absolutely rigid for at least a half hour. I ignored him and went on with the seminar. Finally, he dropped the dumbbell.

I picked it up and switched dumbbells on him. I gave him my special one. Again he snatched it and went rigid. I said, ''Give!'' and he wouldn't budge. So I leaned down and pulled off the one end that was designed to come off and then slid the dumbbell shaft out of his mouth by the other end. The dog was shocked! It didn't hurt him, but he certainly didn't seem very pleased to be holding a mouthful of metal tubing.

After that, when I gave him a standard dumbbell and said ''Give,'' he let go instantly. They never had any more trouble with the Dobe and the dumbbell!

The use of Plumber's Helpers simplifies teaching the Retrieve Over the High Jump. The Utility Bar keeps the dog from ticking the Solid Jump.

12

Jumping Exercises

RETRIEVE OVER THE HIGH JUMP

This exercise requires the dog to go out over the jump, retrieve the dumbbell and return back over the jump to sit squarely in front of the handler. As mentioned before, the dog must be close enough so that the handler can take the dumbbell without stretching or stepping forward to reach it. The dog then goes to the Heel position on command.

In AKC competition, the handler is allowed to give very few commands to accomplish this. Initially, the dog is given a Sit/Stay command. After the handler throws the dumbbell over the High Jump, the dog is given the command Over. The dog retrieves the dumbbell, returns and sits directly in front of the handler. The dog is given the command Give, and finally Heel.

When teaching this exercise, it is very necessary to use additional words and body movement in the beginning. But they should be phased out as quickly as possible.

BREAKING DOWN THE EXERCISE

This exercise is presented to the dog in a series of steps. First, the dog is taught to go out over the High Jump without retrieving the dumbbell. The jump height during training is kept low deliberately. When the dog jumps consistently, you add retrieving the dumbbell and the Finish, and raise the jump height.

AKC regulations set the jump heights for competition. For the smaller breeds, the minimum height is eight inches. The maximum jumping height, no matter the size of the dog, is thirty-six inches.

In order to figure the height your dog must jump, place your hand or a ruler across the dog's shoulders (the withers) and carefully measure the height from the floor to the edge of the ruler. With this information, you can refer to Table 1 for the correct jump height for your dog. Typically, the height that a dog must jump is one and one-quarter times the height of the dog at the withers. There are some breed exceptions, however. See Appendix B for a complete AKC description of these exceptions and the heights they are required to jump.

TAKE YOUR TIME

Take your time when teaching this exercise and keep the jump height low. The dog must have time to focus on developing an approach and timing. If you give her time to become confident in the ability to jump, your dog will develop a genuine enjoyment of the exercise.

Be sure, even at the very beginning, that the dog is centered up on the jump. For this exercise, the handler stays more to the right of center. Keep the dog centered so she doesn't get into the bad habit of jumping off to the side.

Do most of your training at the lower heights. Even if you are tempted to "just see what she can do," don't be in a hurry to raise the jumps. Only after the dog is retrieving the dumbbell and returning to you consistently, is it time to start increasing the heights two inches at a time.

SETTING UP

Set up the Solid Jumps (also called the High Jump) with a four-inch board if you have a small dog. If you are training a larger dog, use an eight-inch board. As you move through the training steps, you

TABLE 1
Required High Jump Heights

Measured Height of Dog at Withers (in inches)	Height to be Jumped (in inches)
Less than 7½	8
7½ to less than 9	10
9 to less than 10½	12
10½ to less than 12	14
12 to less than 13½	16
13½ to less than 15	18
15 to less than 16½	20
16½ to less than 18½	22
18½ to less than 20	24
20 to less than 21½	26
21½ to less than 23	28
23 to less than 24½	30
24½ to less than 26½	32
26½ to less than 28	34
28 or more	36

will also use the number one and two Broad Jump boards placed on either side of the High Jump as a training aid.

Since initially *you* will be jumping along with the dog, practice running up to and over the High Jump without the dog until you are sure of your footing. Move with enthusiasm. When you work with the dog, you want to get her moving briskly, not walking up to the jump and simply stepping over it.

To practice your footing, start about eight feet from the jump, moving briskly toward it. Your right foot must go down six to eight inches from the jump. That way, you will be able to go over the board with your left foot—the guide foot the dog has always followed. Do this a few times until you have your footing under control.

Before you actually begin jumping, put the dog on lead on the collar's dead ring and take her up to the jump to look it over and become familiar with it. Tap it so that she realizes it is solid. Let her look over it to the other side. However, don't allow the dog to walk around the outside of it. Walk her up to the center of the jump. Since the exercise requires that the dog jump *over* the Solid Jump, you don't want to give the dog the slightest encouragement to go around the outside.

Once you are sure of your footing and the dog has been given the opportunity to inspect the jump, you are ready to begin training.

TEACHING THE EXERCISE

Step 1

Use the High Jump (Solid Jump) with a four- or eight-inch board, depending on the size of your dog. With the dog on lead (on the dead ring) at your left side, walk to a spot about ten feet from the jump. Do not give any Heel commands. Just begin moving quickly toward the jump. You want the dog moving at a good speed.

About three feet from the jump, give the command Over. It is important to give the command at the right spot, so, if necessary, place a marker at the three-foot spot as a cue.

When you give the command, give a light snap on the lead, and jump over the hurdle with your left foot. *Do not tighten up on the lead as you go over.* If you do, you will pull the dog off-balance and create problems.

Remember to jump the dog over the *center* of the High Jump.

The handler stays more to the right. When you land on the far side of the jump, keep moving forward. Then turn in an arc and go around the upright back to where you started and repeat the jump. When the dog jumps successfully with you, be sure to praise.

Encouragement and praise are extremely important motivators throughout the training of this particular exercise. Glowering or angry corrections will only intimidate the dog. Since the object of the exercise is for the dog to retrieve and return to the handler, harsh corrections are counterproductive since they will put the dog off and really slow you down.

After several sessions the dog will have developed a rhythm to jumping. When she jumps along with you without problems, don't let her get bored. Move on to the next step.

Step 2

Place the number one and number two Broad Jump boards flat on either side of the High Jump. The number one board is on the near side, the number two board on the far side. Lay them with the higher sides toward the High Jump. This will alter the point at which the dog must take off and creates a longer arc to her jump, which is desirable.

With the dog still on-lead on the dead ring of the collar, start off briskly toward the jump. When you are three feet from the Broad Jump board, give the command Over. Go over with the dog. Always be sure to hold the lead so that there is enough slack. Never use it to pull the dog over the jump. *She must stay centered.* Once she has jumped, keep moving. Turn with the dog and go back to your starting point.

Step 3

In this step, the Broad Jump boards are moved further away from the High Jump so the dog starts to jump even sooner. In effect, this helps the dog control the angle of the arc of the jump so that she is at maximum jump height when *directly over the center of the High Jump.* While this is not a major factor at the lower jump heights used at the beginning of training, it becomes increasingly more important as the jump height is increased.

At the height a dog is required to jump in competition, it is imperative that maximum jump height be reached over the *center* of the High Jump. If the dog reaches the highest point of the jump too early, she may not clear the jump, or may land awkwardly too close to the jump on the far side. On the other hand, if she takes off too late, she has to jump higher more quickly, just to clear the top board. When this happens, dogs frequently use their back legs on the edge of the board to give themselves the extra boost they need to make it over.

Move both Broad Jump boards to a distance of four to six inches from the high jump, depending upon the size of your dog. For a very small dog, you may even want to keep the Broad Jump boards flush to the High Jump.

You are going to add the return over the jump in this step. To do this, you must straddle the Broad Jumps as you call the dog back over. If you have a problem straddling both boards, remove the Broad Jump board on the near side of the jump. It is more important that you are able to stay balanced and back up easily with the dog.

Beginning approximately ten feet from the jump, move along at a brisk pace with the dog on the dead ring. Three feet from the Broad Jump, give the command Over. As the dog goes over the jump, you go over it with your left leg and straddle it. Practice this move without the dog a few times. (You simply put your right foot down about four to six inches from the Broad Jump board and go over the High Jump with your left leg.) As you stand there, you must be sure to let the dog finish the jump and that *all four feet are down*.

Then quickly call the dog by name. Give *no Come command*. Just use the dog's name to get her to turn. As the dog turns, start backing up. *Keep the lead loose. Don't use it to haul the dog back over*. The dog will follow your movement as you go backward. Add encouraging words to keep her with you. Above all, praise when she gets it right.

Once your dog returns over the jumps, you can go back to your original starting point and start the jump again. Repeat the jump several times in each training session until she is doing it right consistently.

Step 4

Here you take a big step forward. The dog performs the jump in exactly the same way as Step 3, except *off lead*. Start eight to ten feet from the jump. With the dog at your left side, head briskly toward the jump. Three feet from the Broad Jump board, give the Over command. As your dog goes over, you straddle the jump. After the dog has finished jumping and all four feet are down, call her name. Back up quickly, so that as she turns toward you, she follows your movement and jumps back over the High Jump. Then break off the exercise and give the dog plenty of praise. Work patiently until she is consistent, but don't practice jumping for prolonged periods of time. Your dog will lose interest and enthusiasm if you press too hard.

Step 5

Now the dumbbell is introduced into the exercise. Since you are also teaching the dog the Retrieve on the Flat exercise, it is reasonable to assume that the dog knows how to retrieve the dumbbell. Still, be patient. Rushing can cause problems and setbacks.

Before you begin, remove the Broad Jump boards and work with just the (High) Solid Jump. Hold the dumbbell in your right hand. With the dog at your side, off-lead, go at a brisk pace toward the jump. Throw the dumbbell and quickly *give the Over command while the dumbbell is in the air*. Notice that you throw the dumbbell *prior* to giving the Over command. Dogs respond well to motion. Therefore, initially, you want to have the dog go after the dumbbell while it is moving. That way you take advantage of this natural tendency (even though this training method must eventually be phased out).

Go over the jump together. If it is too difficult for you to jump with the dog, go around the upright section. As soon as the dog has completed the jump, tell the dog Take It (or whatever command you have chosen). If the dog is reluctant to take the dumbbell, stoop down and give encouragement by saying "Take It, Take It!" If absolutely necessary, pick the dumbbell up and put it in the dog's mouth. Even though the dog retrieves the dumbbell on the flat, when you combine these elements—jumping and retrieving—it may take time to put both parts together. Work patiently and encourage your dog. *No harsh corrections here*!

Once she picks the dumbbell up, make the return jump. If your dog drops the dumbbell, pick it up and put it in her mouth. Make her hold it until she returns back over the jump. Praise effusively, even if every aspect of the jump wasn't perfect. Take your time. Practice this step until the dog is able to do it well. Don't try to rush. If you hurry through a step before the dog has learned it well, you will cause problems.

Step 6

Have the dog sit beside you approximately eight to ten feet from the High Jump. Give the Sit/Stay command. You will continue to throw the dumbbell *before* giving the command Get It. However, in this instance *you are going to remain in place* after throwing the dumbbell over the jump.

Show the dog the dumbbell—slowly move it around in front of her to be sure she is paying attention to it. Then throw it over the jump, and while the dumbbell is still in the air, tell the dog Get It.

In AKC competition, the required distance that the dumbbell must be thrown is at least eight feet beyond the jump. Practice your throws. When you begin, use a marker, if necessary, to help you judge the correct distance.

When given the command, the dog should go over the jump, pick up the dumbbell and return back over the jump. Don't worry about the Sit or Finish. The most important thing is that she went over and back and brought the dumbbell to you.

Tell your dog Give and remove the dumbbell by the sides of the bells. Remember to give praise for her efforts! Don't overwork the jumping. Limit the number of jumps in the practice session. **Keep it fun!** *From the dog's point of view, this should be a great game.*

Step 7

Now, you will practice the exercise as it would be done in competition. You will also begin increasing the jump height by two-inch increments until you reach the height the dog is required to jump in competition.

There is a natural tendency to want to get the dog jumping at full height too quickly. This is a mistake that causes problems. As it is, you will find that you will have to contend with a variety of natural problems that will arise. Don't add to them by moving the jump heights up too quickly.

Sit the dog at the Heel position, eight feet from the high jump. Give the dog a Sit/Stay command. Throw the dumbbell over the jump at least eight feet beyond the jump. Wait a second or two after the dumbbell hits the ground before giving the dog the command Get It.

Once given the command, the dog should take the jump, pick up the dumbbell, make the return jump and come straight to you. Now you can straighten out any problems with Sits. Since you have been training Retrieve on the Flat, there should be minimal problems with the Sit, or even with the Finish for that matter.

On the command Give, take the dumbbell from the bell ends. At this point, you use the dog's name and give the command Heel. You

As you increase the jump heights, the dog cannot see the dumbbell. Throw it where it is easily spotted as the dog goes over the jump.

have now put all the component parts together into the complete exercise.

If at any point the dog balks at the higher jump height, lower it for a time. Then go back up by two-inch increments again until the dog gains the confidence to take the full height consistently. Once your dog has demonstrated that she can jump the required height, do not train consistently at that height. Perhaps one in five jumps should be at the full height. The remainder should be at a slightly lower level. The emphasis should be on precision and the correction of minor problems.

Keep in mind, too, that as the jump heights increase, the dog cannot see the dumbbell on the other side. Do your best to be sure that the dumbbell lands in a spot that is easy for the dog to see as she is going over the jump. Practice throwing it far enough and straight enough so that when the dog finishes the jump, the dumbbell is still out in front of her.

As the dog becomes proficient, you should also begin to vary what you do so that the dog does not begin anticipating commands.

Take into account which way the dog turns after picking up the dumbbell. If to the left, throw the dumbbell slightly to the right. If it is right, throw the dumbbell slightly to the left. It is up to you to be sure the dog is centered for the return jump.

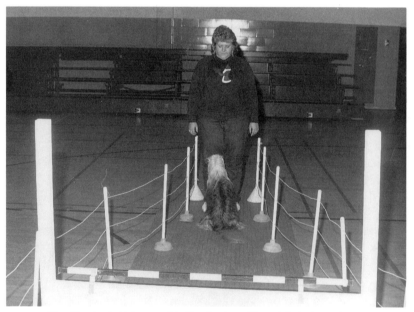

The Plumber's Helpers guide the dog to a Sit straight in front of you.

Break things up periodically by turning and having the dog do a Retrieve on the Flat. Then go back to jumping over the High Jump again.

PROBLEMS

Once the handler remains in place while the dog goes out over the jump, the dog may begin going around the outside of the upright on the return. It is possible, in this case, that you are throwing the dumbbell incorrectly.

Observe which way your dog turns to make the return jump. If, for example, she turns to the left and you've gotten into the habit of throwing the dumbbell too far to the left, the dog will be tempted to go around the jump rather than back over it simply because this path is in her line of vision. Be sure that once she picks up the dumbbell and turns, she is looking at the center of the jump.

If your dog tends to turn to the left, then you should throw the dumbbell slightly to the right. Conversely, if she turns to the right, then throw it slightly to the left. In either case, when your dog looks up and turns after taking the dumbbell, it is up to you to be sure that the jump is directly in front of her.

Plumber's Helpers to the Rescue

Once the dog is jumping off lead, if you wish to avoid any chance of going around the outside of the jump, you can set up the plumber's helpers. This is one of the most helpful training aids you will ever use. They are extremely versatile and can be used in countless training situations where there is a need to guide the dog's direction.

You can set them up on whichever side of the High Jump you may be having problems. If, when going out, the dog starts going around the outside of the uprights, use them to make a chute to keep her lined up on the jump. If she starts going around the outside on the return instead of jumping back over, set them up to funnel the dog back to you. As the dog improves and becomes consistent in returning over the High Jump, gradually spread them wider and wider apart in a fan shape. When you are confident that the dog no longer has a problem, you can remove them completely.

The Utility Bar, when used as a training aid for the High Jump, must be set up on suitable brackets that allow it to fall forward if the dog hits it.

Correcting Jumping Problems

If the dog is ticking the High Jump with her front feet, or pushing off the edge of the board with the rear legs, there are several things you should think about.

First of all, you may have raised the jump heights too rapidly. If so, the dog may not have found the proper angle of takeoff that gives the required height and distance to clear the jump. If this is the case, lower the jump height substantially and slowly build it back up by two-inch increments. If you find the dog is jumping too close to the High Jump, practice with a Broad Jump board laid a few inches in front of the High Jump. If she begins the jump too soon, and doesn't clear the High Jumps cleanly, add a Broad Jump board on the far side as well. If these adjustments do not solve the problem, there are two training aids you can try.

Utility Bar as a Training Aid

Set the brackets on either end of the top board of the High Jump. Place the black-and-white Utility bar on the brackets. (You can

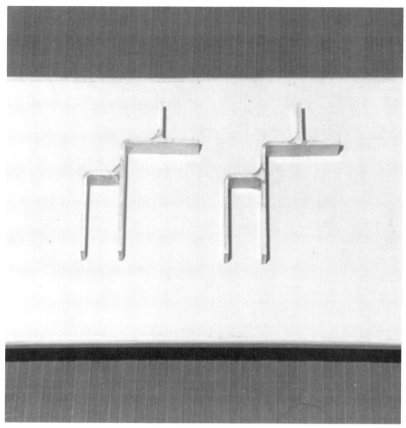

An example of mounting brackets designed to support the Utility Bar when it is used as a training aid.

substitute any long bar. A two-and-one-half-inch dowel of appropriate length works well. The stripes can be made with black tape spaced three inches apart.) Place the bar on the *far side* of the jump. Set up this way the brackets are so designed that if the bar is hit by a dog's legs, it will fall *forward* to the ground. After a few tries, the startling effect of the bar falling is usually enough to motivate the dog to adjust sufficiently to avoid hitting it again.

The mounting brackets shown in the picture are designed in such a way that if the Utility bar is placed on the *near side* of the jump, it then becomes an effective training aid for the dog who attempts to push off the jumps with her rear legs. Set up this way it will fall *backward* as the dog pushes against it. Again, this is usually enough correction to encourage the dog to improve her jump. They can also

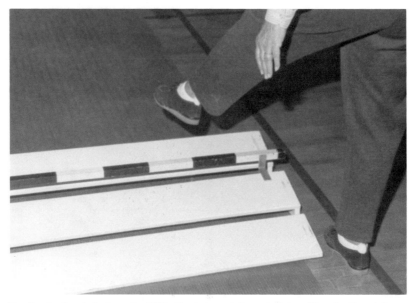

Turning the bracket allows the Utility Bar to be used as a training aid on the Broad Jump as well.

be turned yet another way and used as a training aid on the Broad Jumps as well. As you can see, these brackets are extremely versatile and useful.

If you prefer, try tacking a crepe paper streamer approximately an inch or so above the top board of the high jump. If the dog ticks it, or attempts to push off from it, the paper snaps and create the same unsettling effect as the Utility bar.

THE BROAD JUMP

In this exercise, the dog must remain on Sit/Stay approximately eight to ten feet from the Broad Jump until given a single command to jump.

The handler, after positioning the dog, walks off at an angle to the right side of the jumps and stands facing the jumps with toes approximately two feet away from the boards. The handler may stand anywhere along the jumps from the lowest edge of the first board to the highest edge of the last board.

After the dog is given the command to jump, the handler turns

TABLE 2
Required Broad Jump Distance
and Number of Boards Required

Measured Height of Dog at Withers (in inches)	Distance to be Jumped (in inches)	Number of Boards
Less than 7½	16	2
7½ to less than 9	20	2
9 to less than 10½	24	2
10½ to less than 12	28	3
12 to less than 13½	32	3
13½ to less than 15	36	3
15 to less than 16½	40	3
16½ to less than 18½	44	3
18½ to less than 20	48	4
20 to less than 21½	52	4
21½ to less than 23	56	4
23 to less than 24½	60	4
24½ to less than 26½	64	4
26½ to less than 28	68	4
28 or more	72	4

A dog's eye view of the Broad Jump. From this perspective the stands in the background appear to be very close to the jumps. Also, the jumps appear to be a solid unit. Always allow the dog to examine the jump area *before* starting to train.

right while the dog is in the air. After the dog clears the hurdle, she must immediately return and sit in front of the handler. On command, she then goes to Heel position.

Arranging the Broad Jump—Length

There are four hurdles to the Broad Jump set, each slightly smaller so they telescope into each other for storage and general convenience. The hurdles are numbered from one to four. The highest board is the number four, the lowest is number one.

The distance (length) the dog is required to jump in competition is determined by AKC Obedience Regulations. The dog must Broad Jump over the hurdles a length equal to twice the height jumped in the High Jump exercise. Table 2 gives a listing of the jump requirements and the number of hurdles to be used. This will vary depending on the distance the dog must jump. Suggested construction for the broad jumps will be found in Appendix A.

If your dog is required to jump sixteen to twenty-four inches, use the number one and two boards. If he must jump twenty-eight inches, remove the number four board and use the other three. For a forty-eight-to-seventy-two-inch jump, all four boards are used.

Whatever the distance your dog must jump, arrange the required number of boards so that the distance from the front edge of the first board to the back edge of the last board equals the correct distance the dog must jump. When you set them up, the lowest hurdle is nearest to you, with the low side toward you.

This exercise, like the High Jump, is complex. For the first time when leaving the dog, the handler walks off at an angle. The dog must get used to this change. Also, the dog must learn that after jumping she must turn and immediately return to the handler *without a command*. In the course of the exercise the dog deals with a number of new elements. To help simplify the exercise it is taught in a series of steps.

TEACHING THE EXERCISE

Step 1

Only two boards will be used to begin teaching this exercise. Set out the number one and number two Broad Jump boards, with the lower edges toward you. Place them close together with no space between them. This will prevent the dog from stepping between the boards. Let the dog inspect the boards. You can tap them to show the dog that they are solid.

Use the lead on the dead ring of the collar. Walk your dog back to a position about ten feet from the Broad Jump. Turn, and without a Heel command, move quickly toward the jumps. Keep centered so your dog's line of vision is straight over the middle. The handler stays more to the right. When about three feet from the first board, give the dog the command Over. *Pay attention to your footwork.* Get your right foot down six to eight inches from the jump. Then without breaking stride, jump over the hurdle with your left foot. The dog will follow your movement.

Move energetically! Jumping should be fun for the dog. If she appears reluctant, give a slight tug with the lead for encouragement. As she starts jumping, keep the lead loose so that you do not interfere with your dog's movement. When she goes over the jump, praise, letting her know what a good dog she is! Don't stop moving, however. Circle around and go back to your starting point. Repeat the jump several times so that the dog begins to develop a sense of rhythm. To avoid trouble with your own footwork, practice without the dog.

With this simple arrangement of Broad Jump boards, it should not take more than one or two training sessions to have the dog take the jump with ease, without touching either of the boards.

Step 2

You now spread the two Broad Jump boards a little apart. If your dog is small, spread them two inches, since a small dog in competition may only jump twenty inches overall. If your dog is one of the larger breeds, spread the jumps four to six inches apart, no more. You want the dog to clear the boards right from the start. Don't take a chance on her stepping between them and getting into bad habits.

Again, be careful to position your dog so that she is centered up on the jumps. Keep the middle right in her line of vision.

With the dog still on the dead ring, walk to a point eight to ten feet from the jump. Keep moving at a pace that is faster than normal Heeling. When three feet from the first board, give the command Over. Again, go over the jump with the dog. Be sure your left foot guides her over the two boards. Praise as she lands. Keep moving; go around back to your starting position and repeat the jump several times. Talk and encourage as you go along.

Step 3

In this step, unless your dog is only required to jump two boards, a third hurdle is added. Place the three boards two inches apart.

Whether you will be using two or three boards at this time, insert the dowel bar on the second board. You will find a description of it in the equipment section. The dowel bar will help to insure that the dog gains sufficient height in the arc of the jump so that she clears the boards without touching them. A lot of dogs jump barely high enough to clear the first board. This does not give them enough thrust to clear all the boards. The dowel bar forces them to jump higher and that translates into increased distance.

If the dowel bar were to be placed on the first board, the dog would tend to jump too soon. By placing the dowel bar midway, the dog gets the required height and distance to clear the entire Broad Jump.

If the dog hits the dowel bar, because it is lightweight it simply falls forward. After the dog hits it once or twice, she will adjust her jumping accordingly.

To practice the exercise in this step, have the dog on lead, on the dead ring. Sit the dog centered, approximately five feet from the first board. Starting on your right foot, you will walk out to the end of your lead. Go out at an angle, so that you can position yourself to the right

166

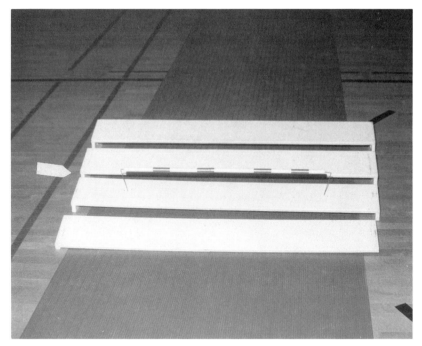

When the dowel training aid is used to help the dog gain height on the Broad Jump, put the dowel on the second board whether you use two, three or four boards.

of the first board. Give the dog the command Over. Keep the lead up and out of the dog's way so it doesn't interfere with movement. As she jumps, turn to your right, facing the same direction the dog is jumping. When she lands, clap your hands. Call to the dog enthusiastically, and as she looks at you, step back a step or two. The dog follows your movement and will come to you in a straight line. Praise enthusiastically every time she gets something right—even if it is not perfect.

Training Aids

After jumping, to prevent the dog from making too wide a circle on the return to you, use the plumber's helpers to make a path. Start them along the left side of the Broad Jumps. Go out past the landing point, and bring them around in a narrow semicircle toward you. This will keep the dog from going out too wide, and will funnel her back to you in a more direct line.

There is another training aid that is useful should the dog begin

To funnel the dog back to you in a direct line on the return, use the Plumber's Helpers for guidance.

walking through the boards. Set up the High Jump uprights with the Bar Jump across it. Place two Broad Jump boards close together on either side with the lower edges toward you.

Step 4

In this step you are going to put the dog on a much longer lead in order to position her eight to ten feet back from the first board. You, therefore, should allow yourself enough lead, so that when she jumps, you're not going to come up short.

As a training aid for the Broad Jump, the Utility Bar can be set up on the pegs of the uprights. Mount the bar on the far side so that it will fall away if the dog hits it.

I recommend that you use a lightweight rope, about fifteen feet or so in length. Attach a lightweight snap swivel to one end. Substitute this lead for the dog's normal six-foot training lead.

Sit the dog eight to ten feet from the jump. With the lead gathered up in your left hand, give the Sit/Stay command. Step off on your right foot, letting out the lead as you move along.

Position yourself to the right of one of the hurdles with your toes approximately two feet back from the edge of the board. Select a spot where you can work comfortably with your dog. How she comes in to you and how big she is, are factors that you must take into consideration. *You want to be a very visible target for the dog.* If your dog is large, don't get too close to the last Broad Jump board. You won't give her enough room to turn and come in for a straight sit.

Be sure you take up any excess rope so that the dog does not get tangled in it. By the same token, don't tighten it up to the point where you pull her off-balance.

Give the dog the command Over. If necessary, give the lead a slight tug, pulling upward and forward. Give plenty of verbal encouragement. As the dog jumps, turn to your right. Once the dog lands, clap your hands and call her name. The dog must come in and sit squarely in front of you. If she fails to sit, or doesn't make a perfect Sit, just back up a few steps so that the dog must reposition. Praise enthusiastically.

When your dog is performing reliably you are ready to move on to the next step. But please take your time. *Don't rush* through these very important steps.

Step 5

Many dogs, when they first come off lead in the Broad Jump exercise, aren't sure what is expected of them. That is the reason for this step.

Position the dog off lead on a Sit/Stay command, approximately eight feet from the jump. Go around to the far side of the Broad Jump. Stand approximately eight feet from the jump and face the dog. *Call her name and give the command Over. At the same time, raise your hands high and clap them.* This will get the dog to look up and better clear the jump. Be enthusiastic! Then take one or two steps back. The verbal command and your movement should be sufficient to have the dog take the jump and come to you. Once she is going over the jump reliably, you are ready to move on to the next step.

Step 6

We are now ready to put the whole exercise together. Position yourself eight to ten feet back from the jumps, with the dog sitting at your side. Give the Sit/Stay command and walk out to the side of the Broad Jump. Take up your position facing the jump with your toes about two feet back from the jump.

Give the dog the command Over. At first you may need to point over the jump to get her moving. This extra cue should be eliminated as soon as possible. As she jumps and while she is in the air, you turn to your right. After the dog lands and turns she can make a direct approach and sit straight in front of you.

Be careful that when you turn you remain two feet from the jumps in order to give the dog sufficient room to finish well. Give the Heel command. Praise the dog. Let her know what a terrific job she is doing.

WIDENING THE JUMPS

You now begin moving the jumps farther apart, if necessary, until you reach the required length your dog must jump in competition. Move them very gradually.

Once the dog is jumping off-lead and the space between the boards is widening, you may have a problem with the dog trying to walk through the spaces. If this occurs, lay newspaper over the jumps. This quickly discourages dogs from this practice. If you have used the dowel bar and moved the jumps apart *slowly*, this problem should rarely arise.

If instead of going over the center of the jump, the dog angles toward the right side and doesn't clear all of the boards, place your foot between the boards and get your body in there to block the area as she jumps. That will move the dog back to center.

If she starts angling to the left and cutting off the boards, position her more to the right on the Sit/Stay. In this way she will be more centered going over the boards.

Utility Training

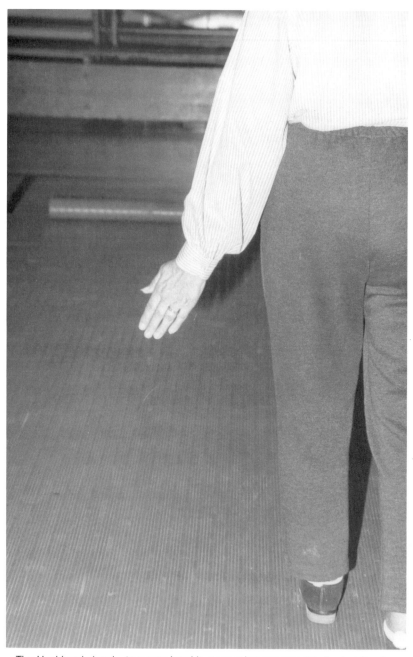

The Heel hand signal—turn your hand in a scooping movement in front of the dog.

13

Setting Your
Sights Even Higher

THERE ARE far fewer dogs competing for the Utility degree (UD) than for either the Novice (CD) degree or the Open (CDX) degree, and with good reason.

The requirements for this degree are much more demanding. Greater responsibility falls to the dog, who must work more independently at this level. Even though the exercises are made up of the basic components from Novice and Open training, they are new exercises, with new elements put together in new ways. They are really a challenge. Judges look at the performance of handler and dog more critically. Because it is an advanced title, they rightfully expect an accomplished, polished presentation. Very few handlers and very few dogs are able to earn a UD degree in the minimum of three shows. Just accept that as a fact of life and Utility training will be much less frustrating.

If you decide to work toward the UD title, be prepared everyday to devote more time to training. Since you must perfect some really demanding exercises, *don't expect to finish this training in eight to ten weeks*.

Continue to practice the Novice and Open routines on-lead as well as off-lead. It is important to work the dog on-lead part of the time so he does not consider being put back on-lead as a punishment. You don't want to create resentment. Just work on-lead occasionally and he will accept it as a normal part of training.

As you review the Novice and Open routines, pay particular attention to Heeling and Open jumping exercises. Use the hand signals whenever appropriate to accustom the dog to them.

Remember to take the time to praise and encourage the dog during Utility training. *Praise is still what makes your dog respond so willingly* and makes all he does for you worth the effort!

Don't set your sights on such a distant goal that you miss the pleasure of your dog's company each day as you train together. Whether the accomplishments are large or small on any given day, enjoy it all. Keep in perspective the fact that the time spent in an AKC show ring can be measured in mere minutes.

EQUIPMENT

Utility level training requires a substantial amount of equipment. You will need a regulation-size High Jump, Broad Jump and Bar Jump. In addition, for the Scent Discrimination exercise you will need a complete set of Scent Discrimination articles, a carrying case for the articles and tongs to handle them. It is also helpful to have a specially constructed scent board for training purposes. A full description of this board is in the Scent Discrimination exercise section. For the Directed Retrieve, three predominantly white work gloves are required.

THE SIGNAL EXERCISE

A Description of the Exercise

This is a challenging, *silent* exercise requiring you to work flawlessly with your dog off-lead. You must work as a team using only hand signals. The dog is required to Heel, Stand, Down, Sit and Come to you, and then Finish. No verbal commands are given, so the exercise requires great concentration on the part of both handler and dog.

Teaching the Exercise

Since hand signals were introduced at the end of Novice training and have been worked on throughout Open training as well, the dog should be familiar with them. When introducing the hand signals, each one was taught separately. Now we will take the separate parts and assemble them together into the Signal Exercise. You will bring together the Heeling portion of the exercise (which is similar to the Heel Free in Open) and the hand signal portion.

OFF-LEAD HEELING WITH HAND SIGNALS

The Heeling part of the exercise is performed with the Solid Jump and Bar Jump already set in place. They are positioned in the middle of the ring approximately twenty feet apart from each other. Therefore, the heeling pattern in this exercise must take this into account.

Begin by standing, with the dog in the Heel position, at least twenty feet back from the two jumps. You should place yourself so that as you Heel forward, you will move in a straight line between the jumps, give the Heel hand signal and begin Heeling the dog forward. Go a few feet and halt. Then start heeling forward again until you are close to the far end of the ring. Make a Right Turn. Go ten to fifteen feet. Do an About-Turn and immediately change your pace to slow. Gradually return your pace to normal. Heel for approximately ten feet farther and do another About-Turn. Change your pace to fast, then normal. Then do an About-Turn, and Heel to the center between the jumps. Make a Left Turn (you are on a midline between the two jumps as you were when you started). Take a few paces forward and halt. This is only a suggested practice pattern. As you train, vary the heeling pattern to put emphasis where your dog needs the most work.

SIGNAL EXERCISE—HAND SIGNALS

With the dog Heeling at a normal pace, give the hand signal Stand (left hand sweeps away from the dog's face) followed by a Stay hand signal (left hand sweeps toward the dog's face). Step off on your right foot, go out approximately ten feet and turn and face your dog.

Give the Down hand signal (right arm raised, hand up, palm toward the dog). Watch your arm and hand movements. Make sure your hand is turned fully outward toward the dog to give a complete visual target. Then drop your hand naturally to your side. If the dog does not respond immediately—move in a step or two toward the dog, bend down slightly and give both the verbal command and hand signal Down. Use an authoritative tone of voice. However, your voice should

The Down hand signal—raise your arm as though stopping traffic. After a second, drop your hand to your side.

remain calm and nonthreatening. Just let your dog know what you expect. Once the dog goes down, praise him.

Keep the dog down for several seconds before giving the next command Sit. Make sure you have the dog's full attention. Call his name so that he focuses on you. Then give the hand signal Sit (hold your left hand slightly away from your body and rotate your wrist with a snapping attention-getting movement). The circular motion of your hand should have enough energy in it to bring the dog up smartly. Be sure as you turn your wrist to show the dog your full palm, not just the tips of your fingers. If the dog responds slowly, or not at all, take a few steps toward him and give the verbal command Sit, immediately followed by the hand signal. Use a firm voice with authority. When he responds, praise him.

Keep the dog in the sitting position for a few seconds. Take your time. You don't want your hand signals coming so quickly he doesn't know what to do next!

After a few seconds have elapsed, give the dog the hand signal Come (extend your right arm fully in a sweeping motion, pause a second and bring it toward your chest with an equally sweeping motion; move your arm as though gathering as much air as possible to yourself). Remember, you can hold the position for no more than a second so make the movement really significant to the dog. Then drop your hand naturally to your side.

If the dog fails to come to you, take a step or two toward him and give the verbal command and hand signal Come. It is important to keep the voice pleasant. Offer encouragement by clapping your hands and repeating the Come command.

Once your dog comes to you, he should sit squarely in front of you. Pause a few seconds, then give the hand signal to go to Heel position (turn the right palm back and then sweep it around in a circular motion). Your dog should respond by moving to the right, around you and up to the Heel position. If the dog does not respond, or begins to move in a confused manner, give the verbal command and hand signal.

Make your movements crisp, not fast. It is more important that they have enough forcefulness to get the dog's attention and clearly make the correct statement.

This routine should be repeated until the dog responds to each hand signal with some degree of precision and consistency. Only then do you begin to increase the distance between you and the dog as you work. Move back in five-foot increments until you reach a distance of twenty feet. Increase the distance slowly. Remember, as you increase

The Sit hand signal—with palm facing to the back, twist your wrist so the palm turns and faces the dog. As you turn it, give your hand enough of a snap to catch the dog's attention. Let the dog see your entire palm, not just your fingertips.

The Come hand signal—as you bring your extended right arm back to you, sweep your hand back to your chest as though drawing as much air as possible toward you.

the distance you lessen your control. It takes you longer to get back to the dog to make a correction, losing some of the effectiveness of the correction. So again it is better to progress slowly.

Once the dog is performing reliably at a distance of twenty feet or so, you can continue to move back in increments until you are working with the dog between thirty and forty feet. This is the distance at which you will be working in competition.

If at any time, the dog fails to perform reliably, reduce the distance. Work closer until the dog improves. Break down the segments and work on them separately. And if you run into a severe problem, there is nothing wrong with putting the dog back on-lead and working out the trouble spots.

Once the dog is performing this exercise well, it is important not to overwork it. Only do the complete exercise routine once or twice a session to keep him focused.

MOVING STAND AND EXAMINATION

A Description of the Exercise

In this exercise, the dog must Heel, Stand and Stay on verbal command or hand Signal by the handler, who is moving. In addition, the judge examines the dog in the same manner as would be done in the conformation ring, with these exceptions: the judge shall not examine the dog's mouth or testicles.

The exercise begins with the dog sitting at the Heel position. On the judge's command Forward, the handler gives a verbal Heel command or hand signal and moves forward several paces. The judge gives the order "Stand Your Dog." The handler gives either a verbal command or hand signal Stand, continues to walk forward a distance of ten to twelve feet and then turns and faces the dog. The judge at this point will make an examination of the dog. Once the examination is completed, the judge will give the order for the handler to call the dog to the Heel position. Using either the hand signal or verbal command Heel, the dog goes directly to the Heel position. *For this exercise only, the dog does not sit in front of the handler before finishing.*

Teaching the Exercise

The exercise can be divided into three parts. The moving dog must stand, accept the examination by the judge and then go directly to the Heel position.

182

MOVING STAND

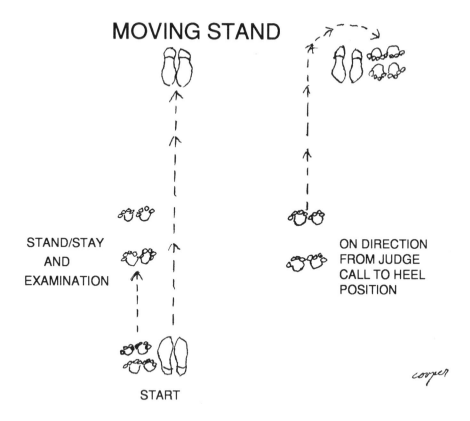

STAND/STAY
AND
EXAMINATION

ON DIRECTION
FROM JUDGE
CALL TO HEEL
POSITION

START

The building block for the first part of the exercise is already in place. It is essentially the same as the Stand in the Signal Exercise. The only difference is that in this instance, the handler does *not* give a Stay command before leaving the dog.

In order to keep the dog from moving after the Stand hand signal, it is essential that you move off on your *right foot* as you leave the dog. As always, *this is a cue to the dog to remain in position.*

In training, if the dog tends to keep moving with you after you give the Stand hand signal or verbal command, turn toward the dog and block his movement. Give both the verbal command and hand signal Stay. Here again, your voice must be authoritative.

Practice walking into a Stand using these extra commands and body movements as long as necessary. Remember, however, they are training techniques that should be dropped as soon as the dog understands what he is required to do. Once you have given the Stand hand signal, go out about ten feet and turn and face the dog. Hold him on the Stand for ten to twenty seconds. Vary the time. Walk back and, for now, go around behind the dog to the Heel position and break off the exercise. Remember to praise.

Next, you will incorporate the Examination into the Stand. Heel the dog forward, give the Stand command and/or hand signal, continue walking and go out ten to twelve feet. Have an assistant approach the dog from the front and examine the dog by going over the dog with his or her hands. The assistant then returns to a position behind and off to one side of the handler.

If on the other hand, an assistant is not available, do the examination yourself. Make sure that after you examine the dog, you return to your exact position and continue with the exercise. It is good to have a number of people, both men and women, go over the dog so that he becomes accustomed to standing in a calm and steadfast manner throughout. By using different people, the dog learns to show neither shyness nor resentment. Once the dog has been examined, keep the dog in the Stand position for several seconds before giving the Come/Heel command. Vary the time. It is important that the dog does not begin to anticipate the next command.

When you are ready to give the Come/Heel command, call your dog by name and give the verbal command Heel and/or hand signal. As the dog gets close to you, step back on your right foot slightly, and at the same time sweep your right hand in a slight arc around your body to the back. These are the same cues you used to teach your dog the Finish in Novice training. These extra cues should be sufficient to get him to move around you to the Heel position.

What you are striving for is to teach the dog that when he is standing and given the Heel command, he should go *directly* to Heel! If he doesn't follow your hand signal to go around you and into the Heel position, put the dog back on-lead. Walk him into a Stand, turn, step in front and face him. Then use the lead to bring your dog around behind you to Heel position as you did in Novice when you taught the Finish. To do that, hold the lead in your right hand and give the dog the verbal command Heel. At the same time step back on your right foot a half step, and guide the dog around your right side. Then transfer the lead to the left hand and guide the dog around behind you to the Heel position at the left. At the same time bring your right foot forward to its original position.

Once the dog understands the exercise, eliminate all of the extra cues and training aids that you have used.

14

Directed Jumping

IN THIS EXERCISE, the dog must go out from the handler in the direction indicated, stop when commanded, jump either the Solid Jump or the Bar Jump as directed and return to the handler. The dog is then sent out again, in an identical manner, but directed over the alternate jump.

The Solid Jump and the Bar Jump are set up in the middle of the ring eighteen to twenty feet apart. The height is the same as required for the dog in Open. The handler is positioned with the dog sitting at the Heel position, at one end of the ring, centered between the jumps twenty feet back from the line of the jumps. On order from the judge, the handler commands and/or signals the dog to go forward at a brisk pace in a straight line to a point approximately twenty feet beyond the jumps. The handler then, without further instructions from the judge, uses the dog's name and gives a Sit command. The dog must stop, turn and sit, focusing attention on the handler. The judge then designates which of the jumps is to be taken first—either the High or Bar Jump.

The handler then gives the command and/or hand signal to the dog to go over the designated jump and return. While the dog is in midair, the handler turns in order to be facing the dog as she lands and returns to the handler.

The dog sits squarely in front of the handler. On command from

In Utility, the dog works more independently *and* at a greater distance from the handler. It is important to train systematically and patiently in order to achieve a reliable performance.

the judge to Finish, the handler gives the command or hand signal Finish. The judge will then say "Exercise finished."

While the dog is again sitting at the Heel position, the judge will ask the handler, "Are you ready?" If the handler's response is yes, the same procedure outlined above will be followed for the second part of the exercise. In this instance the judge will direct the handler to send the dog over the other jump.

TEACHING THE EXERCISE

As you can see, this is a complex exercise to teach because it has so many components. To simplify the teaching of this exercise, it is necessary to present it in several parts.

Introducing the Go Out

To teach the Go Out, I recommend that you use the dog's favorite ball or toy as the incentive to go out. Here, the time you have spent playing will really pay off. We'll teach the exercise using a ball. However, if your dog has a different toy preference, use that. Use whatever will interest her enough to go out.

Walk along with the dog. Then roll the ball out a few feet in front of her. Tell the dog Go or Go Out! I prefer to use Go Out. As you give the command, use your left hand as a pointer. Crouch down a little so you can keep your arm low as you point forward. Stay approximately five feet behind your dog. As she reaches the ball, but *before* she has a chance to pick it up, call her by name and clap your hand, encouraging the dog to turn and look at you. Once she turns, give the verbal command Sit. You can use the hand signal as well for more emphasis. If the dog begins to creep forward, you should move a step or two closer in and repeat the command Sit! Then give the verbal command Stay! Draw this command out to emphasize it. It doesn't matter if the dog sits in a straight line to you or not. The important thing is that she turns and sits.

Then give the dog your release command. Use "Okay!" or "All Done" or whatever expression works for you to break off the routine. Praise and make a big fuss over her. Repeat this routine several times until the dog gets the idea that you want her to turn toward you and sit.

If, when you give the command Go Out after the ball, your dog appears uncertain of what to do, retrieve the ball and roll it again. Don't throw it too quickly. Let the dog see the ball in your hand— bounce it a few times. Then be sure your dog can follow your hand movement as you toss it. Run along up to the ball to keep the dog focused. Clap your hands, talk and be enthusiastic. Many dogs respond quickly to the idea of the Go Out—others take more time to understand, so *be patient*!

Once the dog is going out after the ball, and turning to face you and sitting, increase the distance the dog goes out.

A Modification to the Go Out

You will use the High Jump (Solid) and Bar Jump in the training area. The goal here is to have the dog go out a distance of twenty feet while *you are positioned between the two jumps*, not behind them.

Set up the Solid and Bar Jumps eighteen to twenty feet apart. Position yourself and the dog directly between the jumps, so the dog is not tempted to take one of the jumps while you are trying to teach the Go Out.

Have someone to assist you here. Have your helper stand about ten feet from and facing the dog. Have the other person hold the ball out toward the dog in such a way that the dog can easily see it. Bounce it a few times. Then with a slow, accentuated movement, lower the ball to the ground so the dog cannot possibly miss seeing the ball being put down. Then the assistant moves out of the dog's line of sight.

If you don't have an assistant, put the dog on a Sit/Stay and walk out yourself and bounce the ball and place it down just as deliberately, so the dog cannot fail to see it.

Return to the dog and give the command Go Out! If the dog is slow to go out, start running and in an encouraging voice repeat the command Go Out! Again, as your dog approaches the ball and just before she picks it up, call her by name, clap your hands and, as the dog turns toward you, give the command Sit! The dog need not sit squarely facing you. Repeat this routine until the dog is going out a full twenty feet.

If you have a problem judging the distance, put an unobtrusive marker down at twenty feet. It is important, as you train, to know when the dog has gone out the full twenty feet. If you give the Sit command before the dog has gone the correct distance, you will unintentionally train your dog to come up short.

If the dog begins to go out partway and stops before the twenty-foot mark, move forward five to ten feet and begin the exercise from that point. You should place the ball out at the same spot as before. You then send her to go the shorter distance, using the ball as an incentive. Once the dog is reliable at the shorter distance, back up in small increments until you are sending her from your original position between the jumps.

At this point, there are two methods you can use when placing the ball down. Alternate between placing it down and *leaving* it in place and placing it down and then *removing* it. To remove the ball, bounce it and place it down as before. Then move in front of the ball so that your legs are blocking the dog's view of it. As inconspicuously as possible, stoop and quickly scoop it up and put it in your pocket or palm it without the dog seeing what you've done. Accustom the dog to run out and look for it when sent, whether or not she sees a ball in the distance.

When you call and the dog sits on command, *do not allow any creeping forward*. This is a common problem. If the dog starts to creep forward, repeat the command Stay! Draw out the command to get the most out of it. Your voice should be firm and authoritative, but not angry or threatening! Take a few steps forward to keep the dog in place if necessary.

In competition, the judge makes a deduction in points if the dog comes forward a distance anywhere under two body lengths. If creeping goes farther than that, it is usually a nonqualifying score.

INTRODUCING THE JUMPS

The Solid Jump

To begin this level of training, use both jumps in the training area. Place the Solid Jump to the left and the Bar Jump to the right eighteen to twenty feet apart. Set the Solid Jump at a low jump height.

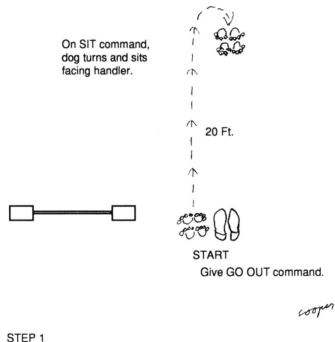

On SIT command, dog turns and sits facing handler.

20 Ft.

START
Give GO OUT command.

STEP 1

INTRODUCING THE SOLID JUMP (A)

Stand to the right of the Solid Jump, with the dog sitting at Heel beside you. Give the GO OUT command and let the dog go out approximately 20 feet. Then, call the dog's name and give a SIT command. The dog should immediately turn and sit facing you.

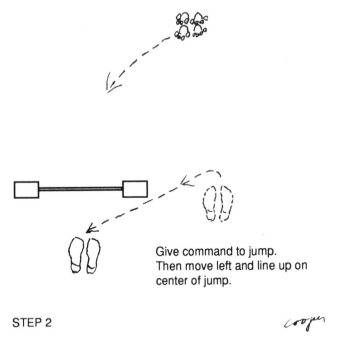

Give command to jump.
Then move left and line up on
center of jump.

STEP 2

cooper

INTRODUCING THE SOLID JUMP (B)

Give the dog a verbal command and hand signal to go over the High Jump. When first teaching the exercise, you then move quickly to the left and line up on the center of the jump as the dog is going toward it. This encourages the dog to go over the correct jump.

Stand to the right of the Solid Jump, with the dog sitting at Heel beside you. Give a Go Out command, and let the dog go out approximately twenty feet. Use your distance marker as a guide. Call the dog's name and give the command Sit! The dog should turn and sit facing you.

Then give the dog a verbal command Over, and at the same time, give the hand signal to go over the High Jump. The hand signal is given by raising the left arm smartly outward to just below shoulder level, palm facing front. Then, as the dog moves forward toward the jump, move quickly over to the left, lining up in front of the jump. You and the dog are then in a direct line. This encourages the dog to go over the jump and come to you. It also makes it clear which jump your dog is to take.

Once the dog has started to jump, but while still in the air, go back to the original spot where the exercise was begun. Once landed, the dog should curve around and go directly to you. In the first phases

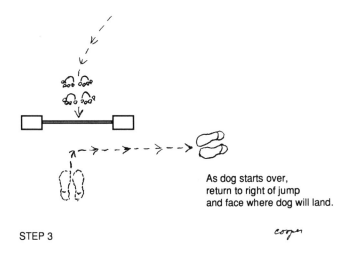

As dog starts over,
return to right of jump
and face where dog will land.

STEP 3

cooper

INTRODUCING THE SOLID JUMP (C)

As the dog is jumping, return quickly to your original spot to the right of the jump. Turn so you are facing toward the place where the dog will land. This encourages the dog to come directly to you.

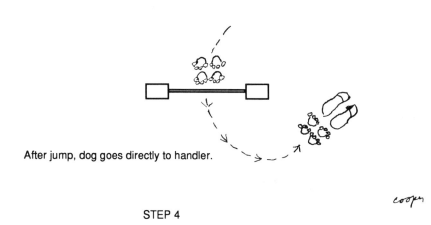

After jump, dog goes directly to handler.

STEP 4

cooper

INTRODUCING THE SOLID JUMP (D)

After jumping, the dog should go directly to the handler. In the early phases of training break off the exercise at this point.

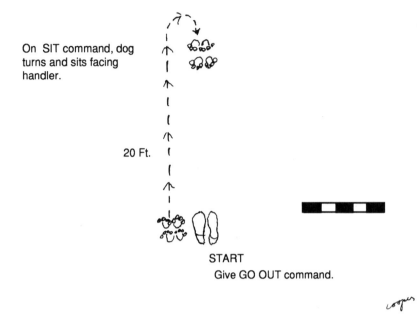

On SIT command, dog turns and sits facing handler.

20 Ft.

START
Give GO OUT command.

STEP 1

INTRODUCING THE BAR JUMP (A)

Stand to the left of the Bar Jump, with the dog sitting at Heel beside you. Give the GO OUT command and let the dog go out approximately 20 feet. Then call the dog's name and give a SIT command. The dog should immediately turn and sit facing you.

of training, I recommend that you break off the exercise at this point. Give lots of praise! Keep it fun so as not to lose the dog's enthusiasm for jumping. Later, you can begin to have her sit squarely in front of you and go to the Heel position on command.

The Bar Jump

Since the Solid Jump was positioned to the left, the Bar Jump is positioned to the right of the starting position. Give a Go Out command. Again, the dog is sent out a distance of approximately twenty feet or so. Then, call the dog's name and give the Sit command. The dog is then given the hand signal and verbal command Over. This time, the hand signal is given by raising the right arm. As the dog moves forward toward the jump, you move to the right so you are in a direct line with the dog.

192

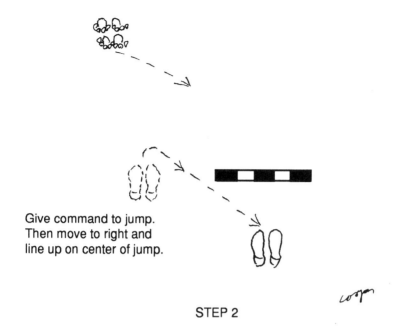

Give command to jump.
Then move to right and
line up on center of jump.

STEP 2

INTRODUCING THE BAR JUMP (B)

Give the dog a verbal command and hand signal to go over the Bar Jump. When first teaching the exercise, you then move quickly to the right and line up on the center of the jump as the dog goes toward it. This encourages the dog to take the correct jump.

While the dog is still in the air, step backward and to the left, back to the spot where the exercise was started. Once landed, the dog should curve around and go directly to you. Break off the exercise at this point. Praise enthusiastically.

Later, you can begin to have your dog sit squarely in front of you and go to the Heel position on command.

COMBINING THE SOLID AND BAR JUMPS

With the dog sitting at your side, stand directly between the two jumps. Give a Go Out command and send the dog out a full distance of twenty feet. Then use the dog's name and give a Sit command. When the dog turns and sits facing you, alternate directing the dog first over one jump, then the other.

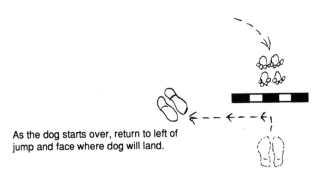

As the dog starts over, return to left of
jump and face where dog will land.

STEP 3

cooper

INTRODUCING THE BAR JUMP (C)

As the dog is jumping, quickly return to your original spot to the left of the jump. Turn so
you are facing toward the place where the dog will land. This encourages your dog to
come directly to you.

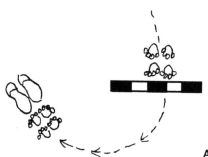

After jump, dog goes directly to handler.

STEP 4

cooper

INTRODUCING THE BAR JUMP (D)

After jumping, the dog should go directly to the handler. In the early phases of training
break off at this point.

194

At first, when you give the signal for the jump on the left, continue to move in front of that jump to help the dog identify which jump you want her to take. When you give the signal for the jump on the right, again move toward that jump to give guidance. In either instance, when the dog is committed to the jump, move back and to the starting position in the center between the two jumps facing the area where the dog will land. Once landed the dog should curve toward the handler and sit squarely in front. On command the dog should go to the Heel position.

If the dog mistakenly goes over the wrong jump, send her back to the Sit position to do it again. Try not to make an issue out of it. Minimize errors and maximize what is right. Keep the dog's enthusiasm and build confidence!

Once the dog is performing reliably, it is time to increase the Go Out to the full distance.

INCREASING THE DISTANCE FOR AKC COMPETITION

The distance of the Go Out should be increased gradually. Begin by positioning yourself with the dog sitting in the Heel position directly between the two jumps. Give the dog the command Go Out, and as the dog is going out, move a few paces backward. The dog should not see you moving back. Repeat the exercise several times at the increased distance. If the dog continues traveling out until you give the Sit command, when she reaches the twenty-foot marker you can keep increasing the distance. If the dog tends to go only partway out, break off the exercise. Bring her back to the starting point and do the exercise again. Don't make an issue out of it and don't reprimand.

It is important to be aware that as soon as you begin to increase the distance by moving backward, the jumps are now in front of the dog who may be tempted to jump over one or the other hurdles. In order to prevent this possibility, set up the plumber's helpers from your starting position to the end post of the jumps. Do this on either side, thus creating a funnel that will keep the dog on course.

Once you have gradually moved backward a distance of twenty feet from the jumps, the dog will be travelling a full forty feet before the Sit—the maximum distance of the Go Out.

As the dog begins to perform reliably, you can remove the plumber's helpers. If she makes too wide a curve after jumping, before the dog returns for the Finish, set the plumber's helpers in a semicircle to guide her into a narrower arc.

It is important during training not to get into the habit of putting the Solid Jump on one particular side and the Bar Jump on the other. A simple way to alternate their positions during each training session is to work from opposite sides. Also, *don't develop fixed habits about which jump the dog takes first.* Vary the choice.

Most handlers will spend a great amount of time teaching the dog this exercise. Most of the time the dog is working at a considerable distance from you and independently. So it is important to train systematically and patiently. Remember this is Utility—the highest achievement in Obedience competition.

15

Directed Retrieve

IN THIS EXERCISE the handler and dog are positioned between the Bar and Solid Jumps with the dog sitting at the Heel position. Three white cotton work gloves are laid out at the far end of the ring *behind them*. One glove is placed in each corner of the ring, approximately three feet out from the corners. The third glove is placed in the center.

When facing the gloves, they are designated one, two and three respectively from left to right. The judge gives the order "One," "Two" or "Three."

The handler gives the command Heel, and then turns in place to face the designated glove. When the handler comes to a Halt, after turning in place, the dog must be sitting in the Heel position. The handler may not touch or reposition the dog if the dog is positioned incorrectly.

Once facing the glove, the handler then sends the dog out by fully extending the left hand toward the glove and also giving a verbal command to retrieve. The handler *may* bend body and knees to the extent necessary in giving the direction to the dog. The expressions frequently used include "Find," "Find It," "Get It" or "Glove."

The dog goes at a brisk trot to retrieve the glove, then comes directly to the handler and sits squarely in front. On order from the judge to "Take It," the handler gives the dog the command Give. The dog *must release the glove without resistance*. On the Finish instruction from the judge, the handler gives the Heel command. The dog goes to the Heel position, sitting squarely.

EQUIPMENT

You will require three cotton work gloves to perform this exercise. The size of the gloves you choose should be governed by the size of the dog.

TEACHING THE EXERCISE

The Go Out taught in the Directed Jumping exercise provides an essential building block already in place as you begin to teach this exercise. If possible, simulate ring conditions by setting up a roped enclosure of approximately fifty by fifty feet.

Step 1

This exercise is introduced to the dog in the same way as the Go Out for the Directed Retrieve.

Work without the jumps in the training area. With the dog walking at your side, while you are holding one of the work gloves, show the dog the glove. Tease him with it a bit to peak interest. Then toss the glove out a few feet. Say "Fetch" or whatever command you have chosen. The dog should go out and pick up the glove without needing much encouragement. Once the dog picks up the glove, give praise. Then call him to you. When you say the command Give, you want him to release the glove immediately without mouthing it. Repeat this a few times.

If the dog won't release the glove (and some dogs won't give it up easily), press your thumb and middle finger against the dog's lower jaw and gently push inward. Take the glove and praise. Don't make an issue out of it. Don't tug on it. It's not a game.

If the dog picks up the glove and begins to mouth it or shake it, quickly go to him and say "Give." Take the glove and then place it back in his mouth again and say "Hold It." Some dogs are very playful and enjoy teasing games. It is important that the dog understand right from the start that the glove is not a play toy. Be sure to get that message across. Once the dog is picking up the glove, holding it well and giving it up on command, it is time to move on to the next step.

Step 2

For this step, work with only one glove. Sit the dog at your side at the Heel position. Have an assistant hold the glove and stand at an angle off to your left and about ten feet in front of you. On a signal from you, the assistant should show the dog the glove, let it drop to the ground and then move back about five feet.

As the assistant lets go of the glove, stoop down, and with a single motion of the left hand and arm, point at the glove. Tell the dog Fetch! Dogs respond well to motion, and by sending the dog *while the glove is still dropping* you provide a further incentive for the dog to go out after it.

Once the dog has gone out, retrieved the glove and returned, praise for a job well done. Again, make sure he doesn't mouth the glove or shake it. If he does, give a correction, remove the glove and make the dog take it again. Don't worry about Sits or Finishes as yet.

Repeat the exercise several times. Then have your assistant move the glove to the opposite side of the training area. This time the assistant will drop the glove while standing at an angle to your right, about ten feet in front of you. Then alternate dropping the glove on either side so that the dog gets accustomed to retrieving from the left and the right.

Finally, still using the single glove, have the assistant drop it directly in front of you, about ten feet away. Have the dog retrieve the glove from this position.

Repeat the exercise several times during each training session. After a few sessions, the dog should begin to retrieve the single glove as directed from any of the three locations.

Step 3

In this step we introduce the Turn Around, sometimes referred to as the Pivot. In competition, at the beginning of the exercise, since the dog and handler are facing away from the gloves, they must turn and line up on the correct one when the judge gives the number of the glove to be retrieved. The handler must turn in place, *without moving from the spot where he or she is standing and line up on the glove.*

This is a real team effort. The dog must remain at the handler's side while the handler turns. You can choose whether to circle to the left or the right. The easiest way for the dog to stay at the Heel position, however, is for the handler to turn to the right. The dog can follow the handler's guide leg more easily. Remember, that when you are facing the gloves, the glove to the far left is glove number one, the center glove is glove number two and the glove to the far right is glove number three.

To teach the turn, only gloves number one and three are used. They are placed approximately twenty feet apart. The dog and handler remain approximately ten feet from the gloves, facing away from them.

Taking the Number One Glove

Assume you have been given the command to take glove number one. Call your dog by name and say "Heel!" Then alternately lift each foot an inch or so off the ground as you move in place, turning to the right until you are directly facing glove number one. With the dog sitting at the Heel position crouch down and give the Go Out verbal command and the hand signal with your left hand. It is important that you extend your arm and hand directly in a line with the glove. This direction is necessary since the dog cannot see the glove as well as you can. When you are standing erect and looking out at the glove, you

DIRECTED RETRIEVE

GLOVE #1

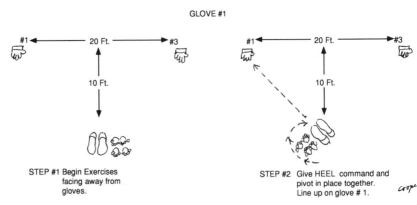

STEP #1 Begin Exercises facing away from gloves.

STEP #2 Give HEEL command and pivot in place together. Line up on glove # 1.

Taking the #1 glove: When you begin the exercise, you are facing away from the gloves. Call the dog by name and give the HEEL command. Then, you both turn in place and line up on glove #1. Next, crouch down and give the GO OUT command and hand signal with your left arm. This gives the dog an accurate line of travel to the glove. Gradually increase the distance back from the glove.

200

are able to see it easily. However, kneel down and look at it from your dog's level. He doesn't have a very good view of it at all. Therefore, your hand direction is vital in order to give the dog an accurate line of travel toward the glove. Also remember that as you go farther away from the gloves, they are even less visible to the dog than at ten feet.

As you give the hand signal, give the command Fetch. Express a great deal of encouragement in order to keep your dog moving at a brisk pace. Once he picks up the glove and turns toward you, take a step or two backward, and if necessary, give a Come command. Don't worry about a Sit or Finish at first. Just concentrate on teaching the dog the principals of the exercise. As he comes to you, tell the dog Give! Once he releases the glove, break off the exercise. Praise and let your dog know he is doing well. Repeat the exercise several times.

If the dog mouths the glove or shakes it, you should quickly take the glove. Then give it back, telling the dog to hold it nicely. Don't allow the dog to tease or develop bad habits.

Taking the Number Three Glove

Alter the exercise described above by taking the number three glove. *The only difference between taking the number one and number three gloves is your foot movement.* Again, call your dog by name,

DIRECTED RETRIEVE

GLOVE #3

STEP #1 Begin Exercises facing away from gloves.

STEP #2 Give HEEL command and pivot in place together. Line up on glove #3.

Taking the #3 glove: When you begin the exercise, you are facing away from the gloves. Call the dog by name and give the HEEL command. Turn in place and line up on glove #3. Next, crouch down and give the GO OUT command and hand signal with your left arm. This direction is needed because, from a lower vantage point, your dog can't see the glove as clearly as you can.

DIRECTED RETRIEVE

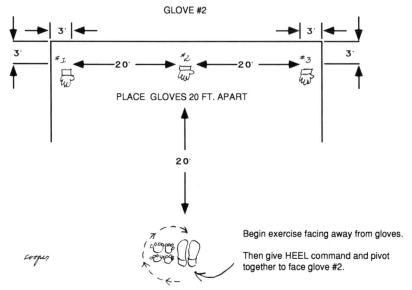

GLOVE #2

PLACE GLOVES 20 FT. APART

3'

20'

20'

Begin exercise facing away from gloves.

Then give HEEL command and pivot together to face glove #2.

Taking the #2 glove: When you begin the exercise you are facing away from the glove. Call the dog by name and give the HEEL command. Turn in place and line up glove #2. Crouch down and give the GO OUT command and hand signal with your left arm. Note that as you increase the distance, the amount of rotation required to line up on the glove lessens. Don't turn too far as you pivot.

saying "Heel," and turn to the right alternately lifting each foot an inch or so off the ground as you turn in place. Continue turning until you are in line with the number three glove. With the dog sitting at the Heel position, give the hand signal and the verbal command Fetch. When your dog brings the glove back, don't forget to praise.

Taking the Number Two Glove

Once the dog is retrieving the number one and three gloves reliably, it is time to add the number two glove. Note from the diagram that the gloves are twenty feet from each other, and the overall distance between the gloves is forty feet. Don't make the exercise more difficult than it need be at this time by placing the articles any closer together.

Again, both handler and dog are turned away from the gloves, approximately ten feet away. Call the dog by name and say "Heel." Turn in place to the right until you are both lined up on the number two glove. The dog sits in the Heel position at your side. Send the dog

202

out with the hand signal and the verbal command. Encourage if need be, and praise your dog for his efforts. Again, do not worry about Sits or Finishes. Repeat the exercise a few times.

Vary your pattern by sending the dog out to each of the gloves in a random manner until he can make a retrieve of any glove without difficulty.

If the dog brings you the wrong glove, don't punish him. Just repeat the exercise again. With the dog working independently more and more, you do not want to make strong corrections when errors occur. This will only reinforce the error in the dog's mind. Just repeat the exercise until he does it correctly. Then praise and show *how pleased you are with what he has done right*!

AN OPTIONAL MODIFICATION TO THE TURN

Up until now, you have been lining up on the gloves by turning to the *right*. Now that you and your dog have gained some proficiency in turning, there is a modification you can make, if you choose. The choice simply rests on your personal feelings, and perhaps more importantly your dog's ability to adapt to this modification.

If you have been given the command to take the number three glove, rather than turning all the way to the right, some handlers prefer to turn to the *left*. In this instance when given the command to take the number three glove, call the dog by name and give the dog the command Back. Turn to the *left*, keeping the dog at the Heel position, and line up on the number three glove. Remember, this is just an option that you may care to use.

INCREASING THE DISTANCE

Once the dog is working reliably with the three gloves at ten feet, it is time to begin to increase the distance. The distance should be increased in five-to-ten-foot increments, depending on your dog's progress. It is better, however, to increase the distance slowly—so that you don't inadvertently introduce unnecessary training problems.

Each time you increase the distance, begin by having an assistant place one glove out at a time as described earlier. Once the dog is retrieving the single glove, the number one and number three gloves can be placed out at a distance of twenty feet. And finally all three gloves can be placed down. Remember the importance of keeping the gloves twenty feet apart.

Once the dog is beginning to perform reliably at this distance, introduce the Sit and Finish commands into the exercise. However, don't do a Sit and Finish every time. Periodically, break off the exercise when you have taken the glove. Vary what you do. Don't let the dog anticipate commands.

As you increase the distance away from the gloves, the amount of rotation required to line up on a glove will be lessened. Therefore, be alert and don't turn too far. In competition, if you have turned too far and find yourself at an off-angle to the glove, you cannot turn back! If you try to do so, it will be considered a second command and you will receive a score of zero.

Once you have moved back in increments and are working solidly at a distance of thirty feet or so, set up the Bar Jump and Solid Jump in their proper positions. Position yourself between the two jumps as you would in competition, and practice sending the dog out to retrieve from this point. The gloves should be laid out twenty feet apart on a line thirty feet away.

16

Scent Discrimination

THE DOG'S SENSE OF SMELL is highly developed. Whether large or small, dogs can detect and discriminate odors with remarkable accuracy.

The dog uses this remarkable capability in many ways and many places, from law enforcement to search and rescue, from Tracking dogs to dogs working in the field. Therefore, it is not surprising that at the Utility level of AKC competition, the dog is required to demonstrate scenting abilities.

This exercise has two parts. The handler must scent two articles, one leather and one metal. In the first part of the exercise the dog must go out and select the single scented article from a group of eight articles. The eight articles laid out consist of four leather and four metal ones, all having the same shape. Once the dog has identified the first scented article, she must bring it directly to the handler. The second article is then laid out among the eight articles and the dog then repeats the exercise, bringing the second scented article back to the handler.

DESCRIPTION OF SCENT ARTICLES
AND EQUIPMENT

There is no hard-and-fast rule about what may be used as scent articles. The leather and metal articles used may be common household objects. Usually, however, special articles are purchased or made for this purpose. Each set (one of leather and one of metal) must consist of five articles. To be well prepared, it is advisable to have at least one extra article of each type.

The leather articles must be constructed in such a way that nothing other than leather is visible, except for whatever metal or metal threads might be necessary to hold them together.

Most handlers find that in the long run it is preferable to buy a set of commercially made articles than to attempt to make them.

The articles come in a variety of shapes, including a dumbbell, a cube, and a triangular shape. They cannot be longer than six inches on any side. Each article should be clearly numbered so they can be identified.

The choice of shape, in my opinion, is a matter of individual taste. Some handlers feel that the cube or the triangular articles have more surface area to hold a scent. I myself prefer the dumbbell-shaped articles. They are easier for the dog to carry and probably emit the same amount of odor as any other shape of the same material.

The two sets of scent articles should be kept in an inexpensive case or some type of container. This will keep them clean and reduce the amount of handling they receive prior to use. It is important not to scent articles unnecessarily prior to using them. You don't want to make the dog's work harder. To handle the articles that are not to be scented you will need a pair of tongs. These tongs will be used in both training and in competition.

Scent Board Training Aid

The scent board is an excellent training aid. It can be of Masonite or a stiff rubber mat measuring approximately two and one-half feet square. Drill two small holes in one edge of the board so that you can attach a leather thong handle to carry it without actually having to touch the surface of the board. Attach ten Velcro strips to the board (one to hold each article). The purpose of the Velcro strips is to hold down unscented articles so that the dog cannot pick them up. Each

The scent board is an excellent training aid. Velcro strips, attached to the board, hold down the unscented articles as the dog begins training for Scent Discrimination.

Velcro strip should be mounted far enough apart so that the articles are spaced at least six inches apart.

THE RING EXERCISE

When the handler is ready to enter the ring to be judged, he or she hands the case containing the articles and the tongs to a steward or judge, depending upon the judge's preference. The steward or the judge, using the tongs, removes two of the articles that will be used in the exercise, one leather and one metal. The selection is usually made by number. If, for example, the judge selects the number three article, both the number three metal and leather are selected (using the tongs). These are usually placed on a clipboard and set aside without being touched by hand. The remaining articles are set out in a designated area by the steward. The steward arranges them randomly. *The steward must touch each of the eight articles as they are laid out.* Both handler and dog are allowed to watch the placement of these articles.

Once the articles have been laid out, on the judge's instruction the handler must turn with back to the articles, and the dog sitting at the heel position. On order from the judge, the handler takes one of the articles designated for use in the exercise and scents it. The handler has the option of selecting either the leather or the metal article first.

Again, on order from the judge, the handler must immediately place the scented article on the judge's clipboard. The judge then places the scented article among the other articles that have already been laid out. At this point, the handler and dog are still facing away from the articles.

Once the scented article has been placed, the judge gives the command Send Your Dog. At this point, the handler gives the Heel command. Both handler and dog turn and face the articles. Before turning, however, the handler has the additional option of giving his or her scent to the dog by gently touching the dog's nose with the palm of one open hand. The handler's hand must return to his or her side before turning to face the articles. Once the handler and dog have turned to face the articles and the dog is seated in the Heel position, the handler then gives the hand signal or verbal command Find It! to the dog.

The dog goes out at a brisk trot directly to the articles. *The dog may take some time (within reason) to select the right article, but must be working continuously.* I have seen dogs that take several minutes to find the right article. Some even pick up an article (the wrong one— which requires a substantial deduction by the judge) and then put it down and continue sniffing through the articles until deciding on the correct one. As long as the dog is actively working in a smart and continuous manner, in all likelihood the judge will allow the dog the extra time required to find the article. If on the other hand, a dog looks puzzled or confused, she will most likely be nonqualified by the judge.

Once the dog has found the article, she returns directly to the handler and sits squarely in front. On the judge's signal or order Take It, the handler gives the command Out or Give, and removes the article from the dog's mouth. The judge will then give the order Finish. At that time the handler gives the dog the command Heel. The judge will then announce that the exercise is completed. The used article is set aside, away from the remaining article to be used. At that time you can praise your dog—but *as in all Utility exercises, only a minimum amount of praise is permitted.*

On the judge's command, the handler with the dog at the Heel position should again turn away from the articles. The handler takes and scents the remaining article. Again, on order from the judge, the scented article is placed on the judge's clipboard. The judge then places

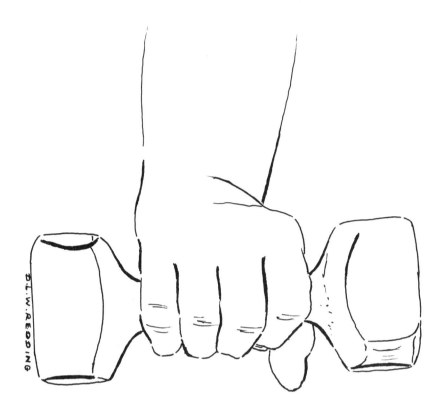

the scented article among the articles laid out, and the exercise is repeated in the same manner as for the first article.

SCENTING THE ARTICLES

The dog's ability to smell is between ten and one hundred times greater than that of humans. As a result, what may seem to us to be a mild odor may be an extremely pungent odor to the dog.

Many people attempt to burn their scent into an article by rubbing it vigorously for long periods of time. This is totally unnecessary. What some handlers don't realize is that the odor may become too strong, and although the dog easily finds the article, *the scent is so strong and changed that she may refuse to pick up the article*! One argument that is put forward in favor of burning in an odor is that by the time the article is scented and placed out for the dog to find, much of the odor is lost. This is not true. Odors do decay in intensity over time, but it takes hours, not minutes.

When you scent your articles bear this in mind. *Don't wring them to death.* All that is required is that you hold the article firmly for fifteen to thirty seconds. I also recommend that if you are right-handed, you scent the article with your left hand. And if you are left-handed, use your right hand. *Studies have shown that your dominant hand may not put as much scent on an article as the nondominant hand.*

CLEANING THE ARTICLES

Once you have completed a training session, you want to remove the scent from the articles so that they will be ready for use at the next training session or Obedience Trial. To clean the articles, place them out in the open air overnight. This is more than adequate to remove unwanted scent. Then, using your tongs, you can place them back into your holding case until you are ready to use them again.

I cannot overemphasize the importance of cleaning the articles between each training session.

TEACHING THE EXERCISE

The exercise is taught in progressive steps, taking the dog from a simple Retrieve of the wooden dumbbell to detecting and discriminating your hand odor on one article placed among a number of unscented articles. Although it seems complicated, your dog should be able to find a scented *leather* article among the unscented articles laid out on the board within two or three training sessions. Each training session should not exceed fifteen to twenty minutes.

Training on *metal* articles may prove to be a more difficult task, taking a bit longer.

Step 1

In this first step you want to get the dog used to working on the scent board. Begin by placing the board, without any articles on it, in an open area. Walk your dog up to the board and let her sniff it. With encouragement, get the dog to walk over it.

Then take the dog back ten feet or so, turn and start walking toward the board. While walking, show the dog a wooden dumbbell and tease her a little bit with it. When you are within a few feet of the board, throw the dumbbell on to the scent board. While the dumbbell is in the air, tell the dog Fetch It or Get It! Remember, dogs follow motion—and you should take advantage of that fact. The dog already knows how to retrieve, and should understand what is required. Once she picks up the dumbbell, praise immediately! Don't worry about having your dog bring the dumbbell back and sit in front of you. She knows how to do that. For now just forget all of those nonessential things. After a few tosses the dog should have no problem retrieving the dumbbell from the board. Now you are ready to move forward to the next step.

Step 2

Now it is best to have someone assist you with the scent training if at all possible. Recognizing that this is not always possible, you can modify these procedures accordingly.

Select one of the leather articles and scent it by holding it in the appropriate hand for fifteen to thirty seconds.

Show the dog the article and tease with it a bit to peak her interest. Then say "Take It." Once she accepts it, praise well. Repeat this a few times.

Once your dog is comfortable taking the article, have your assistant attach an *unscented* leather article to a position on the outer edge of the scent board, using the tongs. Then snap the Velcro strap snugly over it.

Starting about five feet back from the article board, show the dog the scented leather article and briskly move toward the board. As you approach the board, throw the article into the center. Try to place it some distance away from the other secured, unscented article. Once the article hits the board, tell the dog Find It. The dog should go directly to the board (after all, she has seen the article land there) and pick up the scented article. If she sniffs at the secured article, or tries to pick it up, deter and redirect her. If she seems confused as to what you expect, repeat the command Find It. Keep encouraging the dog.

Once she picks up the correct article, take it and really praise for her efforts. Don't worry about coming to you and sitting, just concentrate on getting your dog *to use her nose*. If nothing else, at this point in training, she should begin to learn that the articles that are tied down are not the articles she should be looking for.

Once your dog has succeeded in finding and picking up the scented leather article, you want to *begin placing the scented article closer to the secured, unscented article.* Do this in the same manner described above. The dog should now be able to begin to discriminate between the scented and unscented articles without too much difficulty even if they are within six inches of each other. Once she begins to demonstrate reliable performance, you are ready to move on to the next step.

Step 3

In this step, the task for the dog becomes more complex. To begin, have your assistant secure a second unscented leather article to the outer edge of the board on another Velcro strap. Make sure that the article is handled only with the tongs.

With your dog sitting at the Heel position five feet from the article board, scent a leather article.

If you are working with an assistant, that person should have a clipboard or a book on which to place the article. The assistant should then place the scented article on the board, midway between the two secured articles. Do not handle it or tie it down. The scented articles always remain loose. If you are working alone, put the dog on a Sit/Stay and go out and place the articles on the board yourself.

In either case, once the articles have been positioned, give your dog the command Find It! If she sniffs about and quickly selects the correct article, praise royally and exclaim how great she is!

If the dog attempts to pick up one of the unscented articles that are strapped down, say "Ah-ah!" Encourage her to find the right article. Once she finds it encourage her to pick it up, take it and praise her. Ignore the fact that she went for the wrong one first.

If the dog goes out and seems confused, again give the command Find It. Repeat the command several times, if necessary. Make your voice enthusiastic and give lots of encouragement. Oftentimes, this is all that is necessary to get a dog working. If she still fails to respond, break off the exercise and go back to the first step and begin again. You may be moving too quickly for your dog.

Remember you are working at the Utility level. You are making great demands on your dog, and it may take a little while for her to figure out what you are asking her to do.

Once the dog picks up the scented article fairly quickly, start increasing your distance from the board to approximately ten feet. Continue to use just two unscented articles. However, move them to different positions. In addition, you should begin to place the scented article closer to the unscented articles in order to increase the complexity of the task.

Once the dog is performing reliably, add a third unscented leather article to the board. Repeat the exercise as outlined above.

When the dog is performing reliably with a total of four articles, (three unscented) you are ready to move on to the next step.

Step 4

In this step we are going to begin using the metal articles. Select one of the metal articles and scent it by holding it in the appropriate hand for fifteen to thirty seconds. Show the dog the article and tease with it a bit to get interest up. Then give the command Take It. Once she accepts it, praise well. Repeat this a few times until you are sure the dog is comfortable taking the article.

If you are having difficulty with the dog taking the metal articles, and the articles are shaped like a dumbbell, place a piece of clear plastic tubing over the shaft. This is one of the reasons I prefer the dumbbell shape. Dogs usually do not object to taking the article with the plastic over the shaft. As your dog readily takes the metal article, remove the plastic cover. Once she is comfortable taking the metal article, you want to proceed with the training by repeating the same steps you used with the leather articles.

Once the dog is performing with reasonable reliability, you are ready to move on.

Step 5

In this step you want to begin to use all of the articles together (i.e., both leather and metal). Alternate using both a leather and a metal scented article, so the dog comes to understand that the article she is seeking may be of either type.

You should begin teaching this training exercise at a distance of no greater than five feet from the board. When you send your dog to retrieve an article, give plenty of time to work the board. There are lots of choices now, and you really want her to work hard using the nose only. When she becomes good at finding the correct article and returning to you, increase the distance from the board. Move away from it in a series of steps out to a distance of twenty feet.

Don't be surprised if the increased distance causes your dog some difficulty in finding the scented article. This is natural. If you feel the

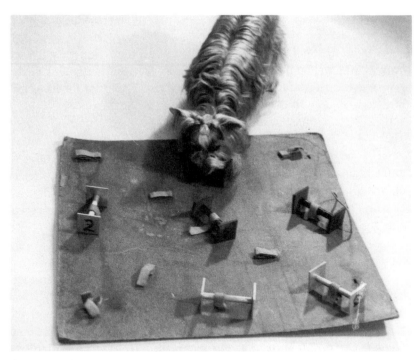

Give plenty of time to work the board when you send the dog to retrieve an article. With more choices, expect your dog to take longer early in training.

dog is really performing poorly and losing confidence, reduce the distance for a while. When she is working well again, gradually increase the distance out to twenty feet.

Don't be in too big a rush at this point. Continue working until you are satisfied that the dog is performing consistently well. When she is, it is time to remove the articles from the training board and place them out on the ground.

Step 6

In this step you are going to introduce some conditions that are similar to those in a show. Select an article to be scented. As in a show, turn your back to the area in which your dog will be working. Apply scent to the article you have chosen. While you are doing this, have your assistant place the nonscented articles out at least six inches apart, in a random manner, using the tongs. You don't want the assistant to touch them. Have the assistant then return to get the article you have scented. Place it on a clipboard or book. *At the start, the scented article should be placed to the outside of the grouping.*

You are still facing away from the area where the articles have been placed. When they have all been positioned, your assistant should give you the command Send Your Dog. Before you turn, gently touch the dog's nose with the palm of your right hand. Then give the dog a verbal Heel command and turn in place with the dog to face the articles. The dog sits. Then give the verbal command Find It!

The dog should go straight out to the articles and start sniffing through them. As long as she keeps working through articles *don't* distract or hurry her along. If she picks up the wrong article, give an ''ah-ah!'' Once the correct article has been found, and brought to you, take it and let your dog know how pleased you are.

Alternate articles so that the dog works with both the leather and the metal.

Once the dog is able to retrieve the scented article without trouble, begin to incorporate a Sit in front and a Finish into your routine. And remember, don't take what your dog does for granted. Always give warm praise for her efforts.

As the dog improves in proficiency, you can begin to place the scented article randomly among the eight unscented articles. You can also begin to move back to a distance of twenty feet, which is the required distance in the AKC Obedience competition.

I cannot overemphasize the need for patience in teaching this exercise. *Take your time and make the exercise fun for your dog*, and you just may be rewarded with an outstanding performance.

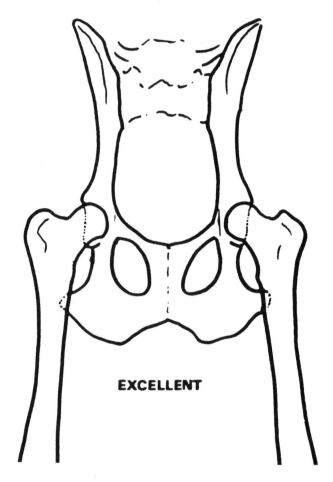

EXCELLENT

This drawing shows an excellent fit of the femoral head into the hip socket. Neither the femoral head nor the socket shows any rough edges, erosion or other irregularities. Courtesy of J. S. Larsen, D.V.M.

17

Canine Hip Dysplasia: Keeping a Balanced Perspective

C ANINE HIP DYSPLASIA is an inherited disease that causes a malformation of the hip joints. It seems to be most prevalent in the large and giant breeds of dogs, and in some of these breeds, it has been estimated that the incidence of hip dysplasia exceeds 50 percent.

There is no cure for hip dysplasia. There are surgical procedures that can alleviate the problem to some extent. However, **the only hope of eliminating it is by the selective breeding of dogs that are certified to be free of the disease.**

Why do we address the problem of hip dysplasia in a book on dog training? First, to dispel the notion that if your dog has dysplasia it must eventually become incapacitated. This is not necessarily the case. And second, and perhaps most important, if your dog is afflicted with this disease, what it means to his future.

In order to do this, it is necessary to acquaint you with a little of the anatomy of the dog.

The hip joint of the dog is that part of the skeletal structure that joins the rear limbs with the pelvis.

It is a rotary joint, a ball and socket, that allows the dog to generate a propelling force to move the dog's body forward, by pushing

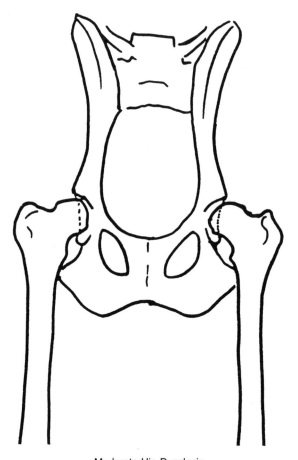

Moderate Hip Dysplasia
This drawing shows both structures changing shape so that the fit is not as tight and compatible as that in the first figure. Courtesy of J. S. Larsen, D.V.M.

against the ground (with one or both hind legs depending upon the gait). The dog then brings the hind leg(s) forward well under his body, and again making contact with the ground, pushing off and repeating the cycle.

This action is dependent upon the ball and socket that make up the hip joint. The ball is the head of the femur bone (the thigh bone), which is smooth and spherical in shape. The socket of the hip joint is the acetabulum, which is a deep, well-formed cavity within which the ball fits. In the unaffected dog, the rotary action is smooth and fluid, resulting in good rear drive and smooth and rhythmic leg action.

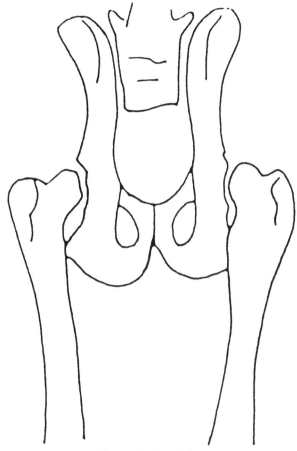

Severe Hip Dysplasia

The femoral heads and sockets are completely separated from one another. The femoral heads are riding on the flattened rims of the socket when the joint is supporting weight. Both structures show a change in shape.

A DESCRIPTION OF DYSPLASIA

In newborn puppies, the hip joints almost always appear normal in X-rays. The bones are still firm and elastic. As a puppy begins to walk, putting stresses on the hip joint, *if there is the slightest lack of contact (called laxity)* between the femoral head and the socket, the stresses begin to cause a change in shape and form of the femoral head, as well as the socket of the pelvis. This in turn stretches the muscles, tendons and ligaments of the hip joint, causing the femoral head to pull away from the socket. As the dog matures and the cartilage turns to bone at about one year of age, there are no further changes in the structure of the hip joint.

In the milder forms of dysplasia, there is only a slight separation of the femoral head and the socket. In severe cases, the femoral head is completely out of the socket.

Figures 1, 2 and 3 show varying degrees of hip joint conformation, ranging from excellent hip joints to severe dysplasia. These line drawings were taken from X-rays of adult dogs.

LET THE DOG DECIDE

Although X-ray detection and classifications are of value to breeders, they are of relatively little value to the average dog owner.

The reason for this is that there are dogs whose X-rays have shown mild degrees of hip dysplasia who could tolerate only a very limited degree of exercise. In contrast, many working dogs whose X-rays would suggest that they could not even walk without discomfort went about their work with ease.

At a more personal level, let me tell a story to which you can readily relate.

Not too long ago, there was a man in one of my training classes with a Golden Retriever. They did extremely well in class, and he decided to work toward a Companion Dog (CD) degree. He got his CD in three straight shows, and placed in the ribbons in several of them. He decided to continue training the dog toward the Companion Dog Excellent (CDX) degree. At the outset, the training went well. Then when he wanted to breed the dog, he arranged for the dog to be X-rayed for hip dysplasia. The man was confident the outcome would be favorable. The dog was a fine specimen, moved well and had good strength and agility. Unfortunately, the X-rays showed that the dog indeed had hip dysplasia. The man immediately decided to stop training for the dog's CDX. He thought it wouldn't be fair to put undue stress that could cause the dog pain.

I suggested that he should *let the dog decide*. Continue training, but with shorter training periods so as not to tire him out. He took my advice and continued training and went on to complete the CDX degree. He also got a Tracking degree! Since then, we have become good friends, and from time to time he reminisces about the advice I gave, to let the dog decide.

This advice is not just to promote success stories. It has a clinical basis in that the dog that is exercised maintains a high muscle mass to pelvic mass ratio, which means that the dog is better able to support his body. Most veterinarians I have discussed this with agree with this philosophy.

If you find yourself in this situation, before you make any decisions about your dog's future, *consult your veterinarian*, and if he or she concurs, then let the dog decide. In many instances you will find that by allowing the dog to do so, you and the dog will enjoy many happy and productive years that you otherwise might have lost.

A Final Thought . . .

DO BE A HAPPY, GOOD SPORT. Remember a 170 qualifying score gets a leg on the degree the same as a top score. Not everyone is a competitor, just enjoying quality time with their four-legged friend.

Well-groomed, friendly teams are a delight to be with and to judge.

Tom Knott

APPENDIX A

Constructing the Jumps

HIGH JUMP CONSTRUCTION

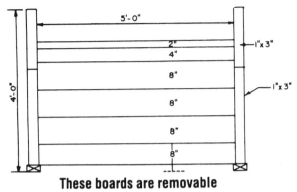

These boards are removable

FRONT VIEW

top view of groove

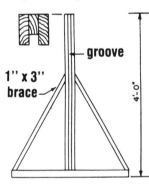

groove

1" x 3"
brace

This upright consists of two pieces 1" x 3" and one piece 1" x 2", nailed together, with the 1" x 2" forming the groove for the boards to slide in.

SIDE VIEW

The high jump must be painted a flat white.

BROAD JUMP CONSTRUCTION

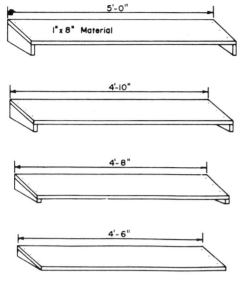

5'-0"

1" x 8" Material

4'-10"

4'-8"

4'-6"

ELEVATION

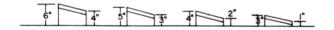

6"   4"   5"   3"   4"   2"   3"   1"

END VIEW OF
FOUR HURDLES

BAR JUMP CONSTRUCTION

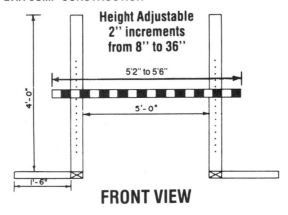

Height Adjustable
2" increments
from 8" to 36"

5'2" to 5'6"

4'-0"

5'-0"

1'-6"

FRONT VIEW

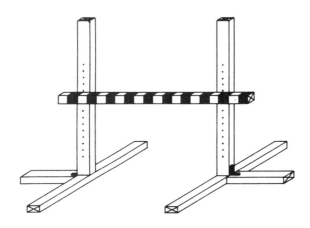

ELEVATION

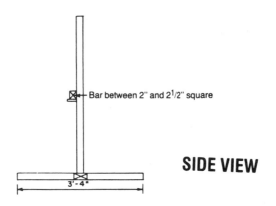

Bar between 2" and 2$^{1}/_{2}$" square

SIDE VIEW

3'-4"

228

APPENDIX B*

Jump Height Exceptions

For the following breeds, the jump heights are to be set to the nearest multiple of two inches to the height of the dog at the withers, or thirty-six inches, whichever is less:

Bloodhounds	Greater Swiss Mountain Dogs
Bernese Mountain Dogs	Mastiffs
Bullmastiffs	Newfoundlands
Great Danes	St. Bernards
Great Pyrenees	

For the following breeds, the jump heights are to be set to the nearest multiple of two inches to the height of the dog at the withers, or eight inches, whichever is greater:

Spaniels (Clumber)	Norfolk Terriers
Spaniels (Sussex)	Norwich Terriers
Basset Hounds	Scottish Terriers

* Reprinted by permission from the AKC Obedience Regulations.

Dachshunds	Sealyham Terriers
Welsh Corgis (Cardigan)	West Highland White Terriers
Welsh Corgis (Pembroke)	Maltese
Australian Terriers	Pekingese
Cairn Terriers	Bulldogs
Dandie Dinmont Terriers	French Bulldogs

For a complete copy of the Obedience Regulations, write to:

The American Kennel Club
51 Madison Avenue
New York, New York 10010